SUCCESS IN COMMODITIES

THE CONGESTION PHASE SYSTEM

SUCCESS IN COMMODITIES

THE CONGESTION PHASE SYSTEM

by
Eugene Nofri
and
Jeanette Nofri Steinberg

Success Publishing
P.O. Box 1995
Santa Monica, CA 90406

Revised Edition

Library of Congress Catalogue Card No. 75-26272

Success Publishing
P.O. Box 1995
Santa Monica, CA 90406

Manufactured in the United States of America

TABLE OF CONTENTS

PART TWO **IF YOU HAVE NEVER TRADED IN COMMODITY FUTURES BEFORE**

PREFACE

When my daughter first approached me with the idea of writing this book, my first response was: "why should I write a book when I can make a year's royalties in the market in one day?" However, after many attempts to convince me to do it, I realized the points she brought up made sense. Since writing this book is a venture mutually advantageous to myself and my fellow commodities traders, I am confident that it is contributing something of value to our society.

The vast majority of people now trading in commodity futures are literally gambling with their money, since they really do not know how to make money in these markets. In an attempt to find out how to be successful, traders spend hundreds of dollars on chart and computer services. Yet, traders lose large sums of money, consistently, because they do not have, or cannot apply, a valid, reliable trading method.

In recent years, the former Commodity Exchange Authority published the results of a survey of commodities traders and their techniques. This survey examined 417,906 futures transactions made by 8,922 grain traders who were "small speculators" over a period of nine years. The CEA report revealed that only 2,184, or 25%, of the speculators had a net profit, and that 6,598 had a net loss.

One might wonder why, with the great profit potential of commodity markets, only 25% came out ahead over the years. There is certainly a plentiful supply of techniques, systems and advisory services, as well as ample opportunity to learn by experience.

As I mentioned earlier, traders have not yet found a valid, reliable system on which to base their trading decisions. By this I mean, a system that is not merely a "theory" that sounds logical, but rather a method that is practical, that *works* when it is put into practice, and that *can* be put into practice. Even many professional speculators and brokers consider futures markets to be mysterious and dangerous, advising novices not to venture into them without a willingness to lose money. Without a sound, practical trading method, commodity speculation seems hopelessly complicated and treacherous. And, indeed, this is true.

If a trader can increase the probability of making successful trades, and decrease the risk of loss, he at least has a chance to see what he can do.

I call the method I have developed over the past 28 years of experience in the market, Congestion Phases. It is a system of short-term buying and selling, based on patterns formed by only a few days' prices.

Trading with Congestion Phases has many advantages: it is a system easy to use, it will protect you from major losses, it can be applied to any commodity and will work regardless of what the short, medium or long range trend is. It has proved reliable through every type of fundamental or technical happening – crop damage, foreign sales, rumors of war, peace, market corrections, support levels, etc. No matter what else is going on, the Congestion Phase System will prove its profit ability.

Eugene Nofri

INTRODUCTION

In 1946 I was voted to the Chicago Board of Trade with an account balance of $800. This set a record for the poorest member ever voted to the "big board." At that time, I had a wife and three children to support. With such meager financing, I was hardly in a position to engage in risky speculation. I simply couldn't afford to lose. Yet, my fascination with the commodity markets and the opportunity for making big money was too much to pass up. I could have settled for an ordinary job but I had big dreams and futures speculation seemed like the perfect way to make them come true.

Through trial and error, and a strong determination to discover a way to predict how prices will move, I developed Congestion Phases. To show how it continues to work throughout the years, I offer the following excerpt from my experience with this system.

In August of 1972 I bought future contracts of wheat, plywood, soybeans, soybean oil, meal and silver by putting up $45,000 on margin (about 10% of the total value of the contracts). The day after I bought the wheat, the price went up the limit. The limit on wheat, at that time, was 10 cents, and since I had bought 50,000 bushels, my profit, on paper, was $5,000. According to my chart, the Congestion Phase told me that the chances were very good that the price would go up again the following day, so I held on. The next day, the price went up the limit again. At the end of the second day I sold my 10 contracts, according to my system, at the day's closing price for a two-day profit of $9,800. My profit between August and October averaged from $2,000 to $8,000 *a day*. And on one of the days, I made $18,000 on *one trade*.

Within that two-month period, I traded with a profit *every day for 45 days straight*. By the time I got out of the market at the end of October, I had doubled my starting capital for a net profit of $90,000.

We all know that there is big money to be made in futures markets. It may not be unusual for a trader to double his money within a month, or even a few weeks. What is unusual, is to continue to be successful over a long period of time.

Trading with Congestion Phases has proven to be close to 75% effective as a guide to making profitable trades.

By their own admission, the biggest problem for commodities traders in knowing *when* to buy and *when* to sell. It may not be too difficult to predict which direction the trend is headed, or that it will reverse in the near future. But in order to make a profitable trade, the correct action must be taken at the right time.

I'm sure it is safe to assume that every trader has this as his objective. But most are simply guessing or playing their hunches. Certainly luck does play a part in making money in any medium, but sometimes our luck runs out.

When my luck was at an ebb, I was always able to cut my losses to a minimum. Congestion Phases saw me through the rough time satisfactorily.

The excitement of floor trading is always vividly alive in my mind. The market is part of what has made my life interesting and worthwhile.

It is my hope that the use of my Congestion Phase System will cause many traders, who do not already think so, to discover that commodities can be fun!

PART ONE

THE CONGESTION PHASE SYSTEM

HOW THE CONGESTION PHASE SYSTEM WORKS

The Congestion Phase System is made up of thirty-two "phases" or patterns which appear at least 75% of the time during periods of market congestion. Phases appear in both uptrends and downtrends and are usually determined by a two or more consecutive day move in one direction.

The repetitive occurance of phases and predictability of price movement immediately following them is what gives the Congestion Phase system its reliability. The trading instructions which accompany the illustrations of the phases in the next chapter are based apon that statistical probability. Congestion Phases have proven reliable more than 75% of the time over the twenty-five years I have used them.

This system of trading can be used in two ways; for "scalping" quick profits and for profit-taking advice when a position is already held in the market based on some other method of speculation.

The term "scalping" as used with this system means to get in and out of the market quickly, taking relatively smaller profits. However, the profit made with this System will be more consistent than with any other method, as well as limiting the size of losses.

If you wish to use the Congestion Phase System in conjunction with the method you are now using, it is very feasible to do so. A common problem, admitted to by both the

Figure 1

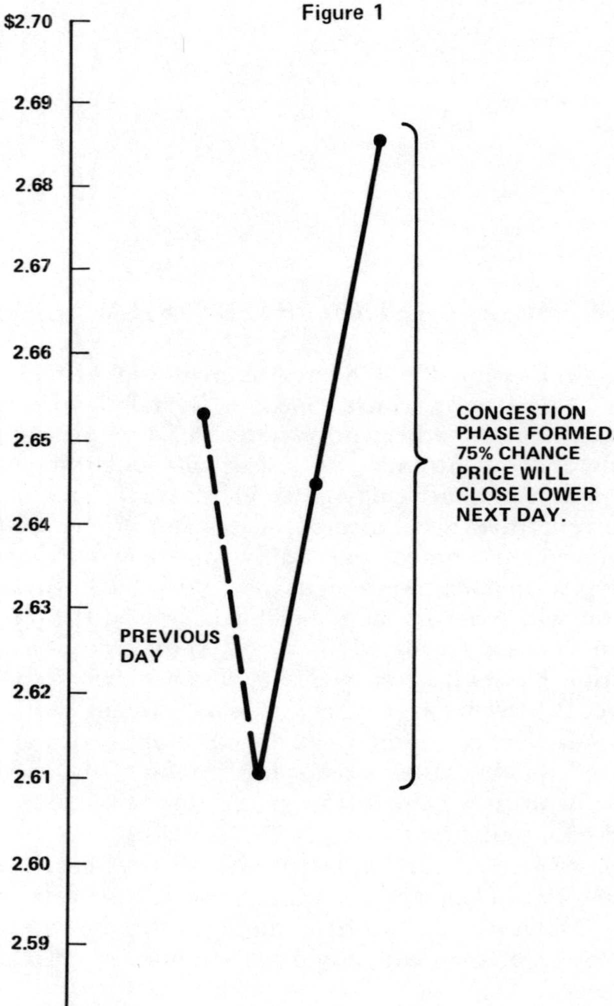
$2.70
2.69
2.68
2.67
2.66
2.65
2.64
2.63
2.62
2.61
2.60
2.59
2.58
PREVIOUS
DAY
CONGESTION
PHASE FORMED.
75% CHANCE
PRICE WILL
CLOSE LOWER
NEXT DAY.

professional and casual commodity trader is knowing exactly when to take profits. Getting out of the market is often based on guess work. Congestion Phases, however, will tell you the best time to close out a position, once you have decided to do so. This will be explained in more detail in the next Chapter.

The principle behind the predictability of Congestion Phases is based on the pressure, and counter-pressure, of buying and selling. This is explained in Chapter 4, "Rally and Reaction", but simply stated, after the appearance of a Congestion Phase there is a high probability that on the following day the price will go in the opposite direction of the phase that has just formed. For example, if the price closes higher than the previous day's close two days in a row it has formed a phase. The formation of this phase means that on the third day there is about a 75% chance that the price will close lower than the second day's closing price.

A two consecutive day move is the most common Congestion Phase. It can be used on its own, or may become part of other phases, depending upon subsequent closing prices. All thirty-two phases, along with trading instructions, appear in the next chapter.

The Congestion Phase System, then, is a method of commodities trading by which you consult a chart of closing prices, determined to be in a period of market congestion, and identify a current pattern as a Congestion Phase. When a Congestion Phase forms, the trading instructions given for that phase can be used by the trader. Trading according to Congestion Phases, give the trader about a 75% chance of making a profitable trade.

Before actually beginning to trade with the Congestion Phase System you will need a chart of the closing prices of the commodity you wish to trade in and you must then identify a current period of market congestion.

Charting Closing Prices

Since commodity prices are usually plotted on a graph showing the high, low and closing price of each trading day, it is unorthodox to plot a commodity's closing prices exclusively. I will explain why only the closing prices are necessary for success with the Congestion Phase System.

This system is based on price movements, *not on the actual prices reached by a commodity.* It is, in fact, not possible to predict an exact price a commodity will reach at a given time. You may have had the experience of placing an order at a specific price, only to miss it by a fraction; or perhaps it did hit the price for one or two trades, but your order was not filled. All we really know about commodity prices is that *they fluctuate.*

The high, low and closing prices of a commodity run in the same general direction; i.e., conform similarly to buying and selling pressure. The following illustration shows the high, low and closing prices for July 1975 corn. As you can see, the three lines form patterns which are similar enough to conclude that each reflects market pressure about the same.

It is also an advantage to plot only closing prices because it is simpler, less time consuming and easier to read than any other type of charting method.

Since daily closing prices reflect the buying and selling pressure of the market on their own, it is a simple matter to plot the closing prices on a chart and connect the dots. If, however, you already plot all three prices in your chart, you can continue to do so if you wish and simply connect the closing prices to aid in determining when a Congestion Phase appears. You may wish to refer to Chapter 10, Part II which gives the new trader step-by-step instructions on how to make a Congestion Phase chart.

Figure 2
CORN, July 1975

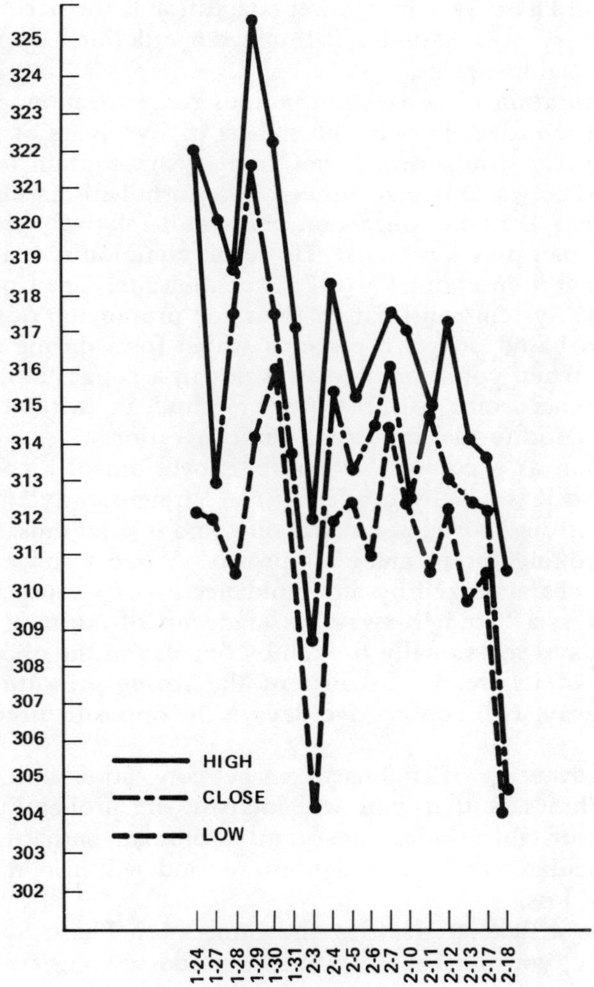

Identifying Market Congestion

The term "congestion" is sometimes used in relation to supply and demand and technical theories. As used with the Congestion Phase System, market congestion is the occurance of temporary price stability within a range defined by a specific high and low price.

The duration of congestion periods range from one week to several months. Looking at a chart of five years of commodity prices would reveal that some years contain longer periods of congestion than others. The turbulent markets of recent years contain congestion periods of relatively shorter duration than previous years. However, commodity markets are in congestion about 65 to 75% of the time. The Congestion Phase System can be used the same proportion of time, since it is based on price patterns which form during these periods. When your commodity is not in a congestion, you may trade according to some other method, or switch to another commodity that is currently in congestion.

As soon as a commodity's price moves out of a congestion period it is usually headed into a "straight-away" move. This is a strong move in one direction, and is what most traders are looking for to make big profits. While a congestion period is characterized by an abundance of two consecutive days moves, a "straight-away" is made up of multiple consecutive days occasionally broken by one day in the opposite direction of its trend. Because of the strong pressure of a straight-away, two consecutive days in the opposite direction is rare.

The advantage of trading in market congestion with Congestion Phases is that you will increase the probability of making profitable trades consistently, though, perhaps, not so spectacularly as in a straight-away, and will also reduce the risk of loss.

If you wish to trade with the Congestion Phase System exclusively, you must wait until a commodity congests after a straight-away move, or you can switch to another commodity that is currently in a congestion period. If you wish to use another method of trading when a commodity is not in congestion, it is feasible to do so. In fact, Congestion Phases can be used together with fundamental and technical analysis because Congestion Phases are simply a way to get quickly in and out of the market profitable.

In order to explain how to identify a congestion period, I will use two charts; one containing a congestion lasting eighteen days and the other lasting seven days.

For the purpose of illustration, these example charts are presented as a situation where a new chart is being made. However, the same principles apply to identifying a congestion period in a chart you are already keeping or one made by a charting service.

When beginning to plot a new commodity in order to determine if it is in a congestion period, you must record at least ten days' closing prices on your chart. If a congestion is not indicated after ten days, continue to plot until it is. You may wish to plot several commodities simultaneously in order to be able to trade in one commodity while waiting for another to congest.

In the following charts, the top and bottom of the congestion are labeled and marked with an arrow and each day's closing price is indicated by a heavy black dot for easy reading. I will first state the Congestion Rule and then proceed to show how to find a congestion period in your chart.

CONGESTION RULE:

> When a high and low price in your chart is not broken through by subsequent closing prices, and are both immediately followed by two consecutive closing prices in the opposite direction, the commodity can be said to be in a period of market congestion.

Figure 3

WHEAT, May 1973
CONGESTION

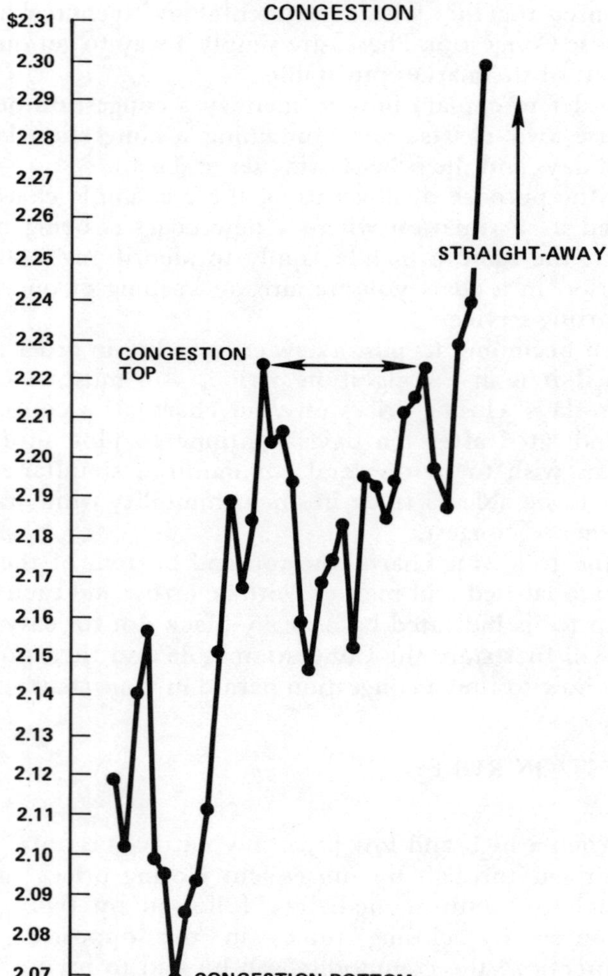

> Until either the top or bottom boundary of the congestion is broken through by two consecutive days beyond the highest or lowest closing price already plotted in the chart, it is in a period in which Congestion Phases can be used.

In my first example chart, after plotting ten days of closing prices, the bottom of the congestion is established because the low price of $2.07 is immediately followed by two consecutive closing prices in the opposite direction and has not been broken through by a lower price. At this point, we must continue to plot closing prices until a congestion top is formed. After plotting the thirteenth day it may look like $2.19 will be the top. However, there is only one day in the opposite direction following this price. If on the fourteenth day the price closed lower than $2.17 the congestion would have been established, but it did not. Instead, the price moved beyond $2.19 to $2.22½. On the 16th and 17th days the prices are within ½-cent of each other and are, therefore, considered to be the same price (this rule applies throughout the Congestion Phase System). The eighteenth day, at a closing price of $2.19¾ counts as the second consecutive day lower than the top, and thereby establishing that a period of market congestion has occured.

The 33rd day plotted on this chart (the eighteenth day of congestion period) is the last closing price of this congestion period. The next day the price moves beyond the top of $2.22½ to $2.23. If the price had moved downward the next trading day, back into the established congestion period, $2.23 would have been the new top of the congestion with $2.04 remaining the bottom.

However, the following day the price closed higher again, for a second consecutive day, ending the congestion period it had just broken through. This breaking out of a stable period is called a "straight-away." It is characterized by multiple days in one direction with an occasional single day

Figure 4

SOYBEANS, May 1975
CONGESTION

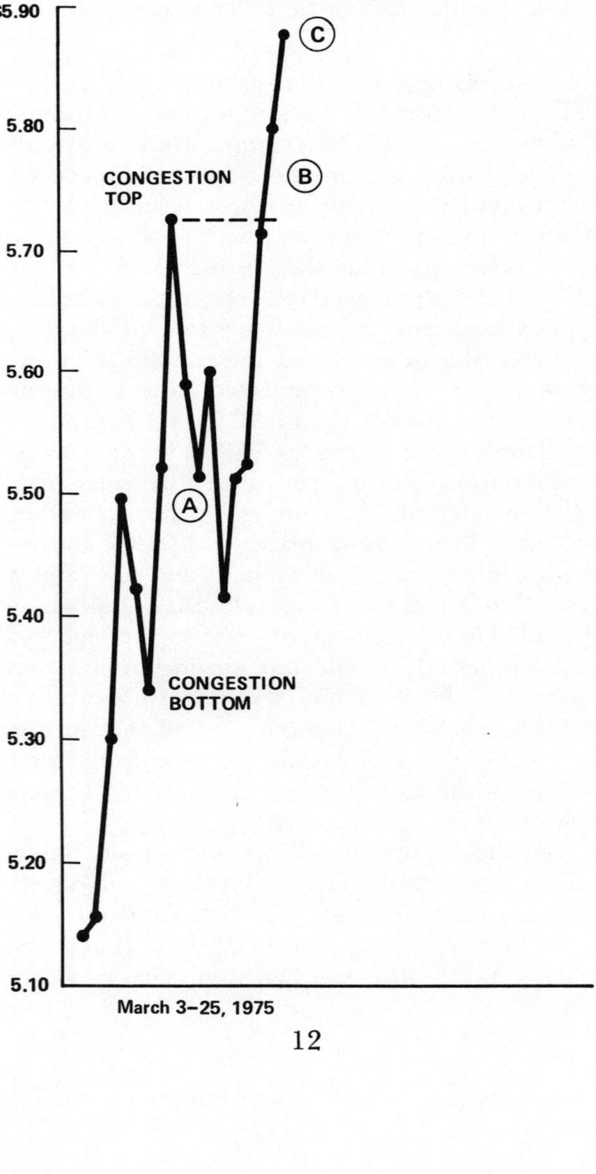

in the opposite direction of its trend. Congestion phases are not applicable in a straight-away.

The second example chart of market congestion shows a congestion of a relative short period of time, seven trading days. In this chart, the tenth day's closing price plotted on the graph, (A), is the point at which the congestion is verified because a previous low is followed by two consecutive days up, and the highest closing price is followed by two days down. The congestion is broken through on the eighth day, (B), and the second consecutive higher close on the ninth day, (C), ends the congestion period.

I have suggested plotting a minimum of ten days' previous closing prices because this is *usually* enough time, in today's market, to identify a congestion period. However, the more prices you plot the better picture you will have of the status of a commodity's current price. Plotting one or two months of previous closing prices is not a bad idea.

NOTE:

> If a "straight-away" occurs in your chart (multiple days in one direction with an occasional single day in the opposite direction) continue to plot closing prices until a bottom and top is reached, followed by two consecutive days in the opposite direction, thus verifying a new congestion period.

It is possible that a commodity you are charting has just passed out of a congestion when you begin recording it in your chart. Do not feel frustrated that you have missed out; there will always be congestion periods forming in your chart. Always plot *previous* prices from a charting service or some other source so that, if necessary, you can act immediately if the current status of your commodity calls for it.

On occasion, a price may break through the top or bottom of a congestion and then reverse with two consecutive

Figure 5

SILVER (CHICAGO), June 1975

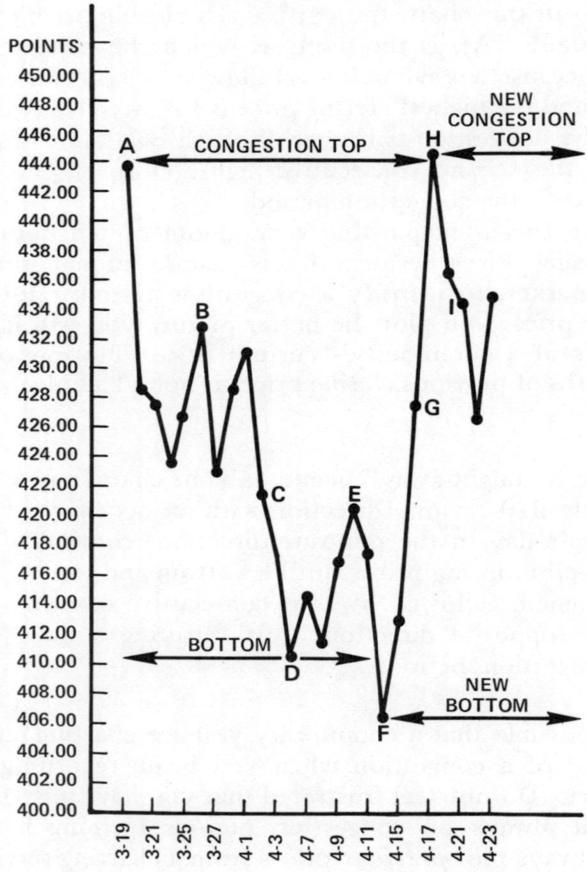

days back into the congestion. If this happens, use the new high or low price as an upper or lower limit of a new congestion period, keeping the former opposite limit as the boundary of the new congestion. For example, in Figure 5, June, 1975 Chicago Silver, the congestion top of 443.75 points (A) was broken through on April 17 (H). This break is followed by two consecutive days' closes back into the congestion (I), which confirms 444.25 as the new top of the congestion period.

Let's go through this Silver chart, step by step, as a trader plotting closing prices in search of a congestion period.

After recording 10 days of closing prices (C), we can see that 443.75 (A) seems to be the top limit of this time period; confirmed by the following two consecutive days down. We continue entering closing prices in order to establish a bottom limit to the congestion period. This happens on April 10 (E), which verifies that 410.25 points is the lowest price for the period (D).

On April 14, 406.25 is recorded in the chart (F). When we plot two more closing prices (G), 406.25 is confirmed as a new bottom of the congestion period.

As mentioned earlier, on April 17 (H) a new top boundary was formed, confirmed on April 21 (I) the second consecutive day back into the already established congestion period.

If you will go through some old charts looking for congestion periods, you will be able to identify them with little trouble. Once you understand what a congestion period looks like and how to identify one, you are ready to look for Congestion Phases and begin trading.

TRADING WITH CONGESTION PHASES

Understanding Congestion Phases

The following thirty-two Congestion Phases appear with regularity during periods of market congestion. They are numbered from one to thirty-two for convenience.

The first eight Phases are comprised of closing prices moving in a downward direction, and the second eight are closing prices moving in an upward pattern. Phases #17 through 32 are *Double Phases*, or simple, one Congestion Phase immediately followed by, or combined with another Congestion Phase.

The amount of price change as shown in Congestion Phases is representative only. Naturally, the actual price changes in your chart will not, necessarily, coincide with those of the Phases. But the general pattern of fluctuation, as well as the proportion, should conform closely to the Congestion Phases illustrated.

For example, Phase #1 is a three consecutive day move down. It is illustrated as one big day down followed by a small day and a third big day down. If the pattern in your chart is three limit days down or three small days down, they are the same pattern as Congestion Phase #1. In Phase #5 the proportion of change is a key factor. The second day's closing price is higher than the first day's *but not higher than the top of the Phase*; and the third day's closing price is lower than the first day's lower close. Regardless of how much a commodity's price fluctuates, if it forms a similar pattern and proportion to Phase #5, it can be considered to be that Phase and trading can commence according to the trading instructions for that particular Phase.

For simplification, separate Phase numbers are given to different proportions of the same Phase as in Phase #2 and #6 which are both comprised of two consecutive days down; Phase #2 is one big day down followed by a small day down, and Phase #6 is one small day down followed by a big day down.

Phases #18 and #26 both contain a closing price that represents no change from the previous day's price. In this case, you would not count the day the price did not change. These two Phases then, should be considered four day Phases. In fact, if the price ever closes ½-cent or less from a previous day's close it should not be counted as a day's move.*

NOTE:

> In a market characterized by very small daily price changes, a limit move in one day is considered to be two days' worth of movement and, therefore, can be used as a two day Phase.

Each day's closing price is indicated by a heavy black dot for easier reading. The point of action in each Congestion

*Unless occuring in a conservatively-moving market when ½-cent moves are a daily happening.

CONGESTION PHASES
#1 thru #8
Downtrend

For an existing SHORT position: Take profit or cover position by *buying* at the bottom of the Phase (circled).

To scalp: Buy at the bottom of the Phase (circled) then *sell* on the close of the first day up from a previous day's close.

NO. 1 **NO. 2** **NO. 3** **NO. 4**

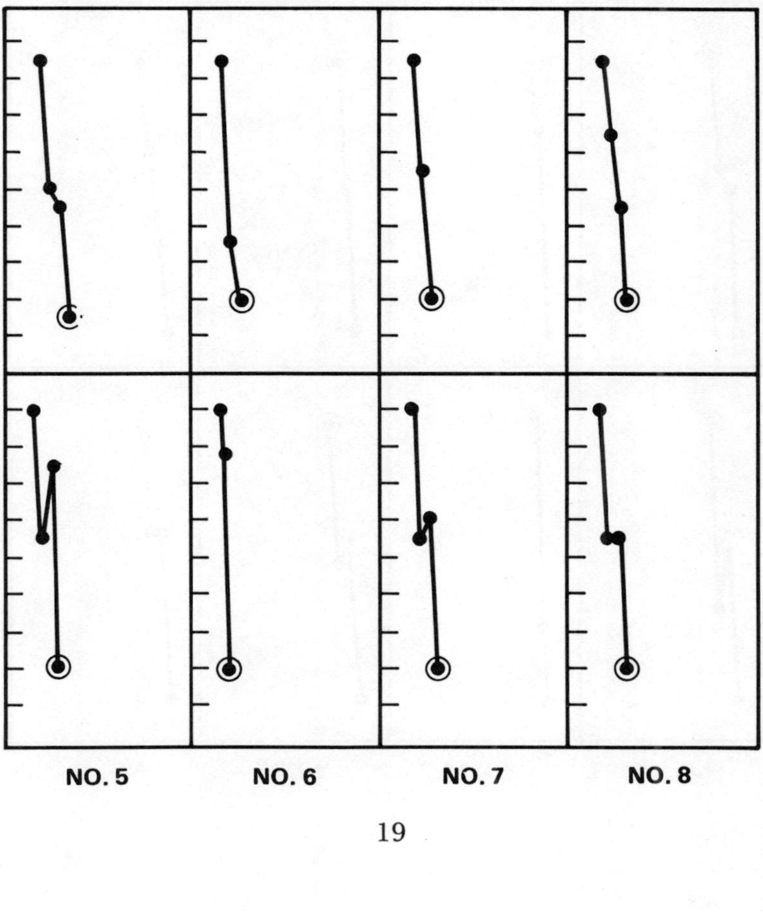

NO. 5 **NO. 6** **NO. 7** **NO. 8**

CONGESTION PHASES
#9 thru #16
Uptrend

For an existing LONG position: Take profit or cover position by *selling* at the top of the Phase.

To scalp: *Sell* at the top of the Phase; then *buy* on the close of the first day down from a previous day's close.

NO. 9 **NO. 10** **NO. 11** **NO. 12**

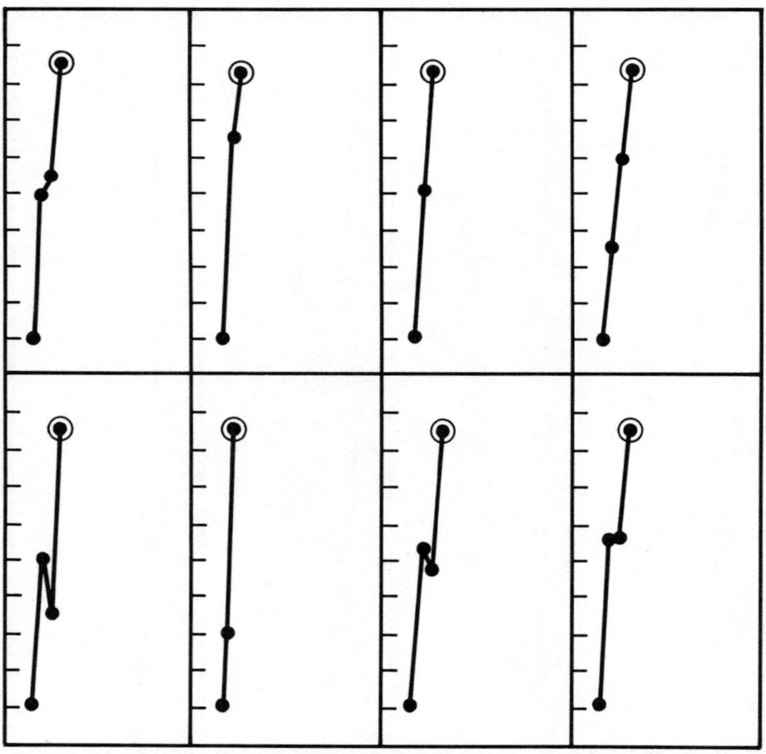

NO. 13 **NO. 14** **NO. 15** **NO. 16**

Phase is circled. The beginning dot of each Phase is the closing price of the previous day which closed in the opposite direction of the Phase just forming.

Once the Congestion Phases are identified in your chart by matching their patterns with those in your chart, you should follow the instruction given for that Phase.

Double Phases

Sometimes Congestion Phases appear one immediately after the other or combined together with a common day. Congestion Phases #17 through #24 are Double Phases in a downtrend and Phases #25 through #32 are Double Phases moving upward.

Since a Double Phase represents twice as much buying or selling pressure as a single Phase, the movement after a Double Phase has formed will be twice that which follows a single Phase. In other words, since there is a high probability that after a two consecutive day move the third day will go in the reverse direction, after a Double Phase occurs, there is a high probability that the price will move in the opposite direction of the Phase two days in a row.

NOTE:

> When a single Phase pattern melts into a Double Phase before the trade is completed, the trading instructions for the Double Phase should be followed *instead of* the instructions for the original single Phase.

DOUBLE CONGESTION PHASES
#17 thru #24
Downtrend

For an existing SHORT position: Take profit or cover position by *buying* at the bottom of the Phase.

To scalp: Buy at bottom of Phase; then *sell* on the close of a second consecutive day up.

NO. 17 NO. 18 NO. 19 NO. 20

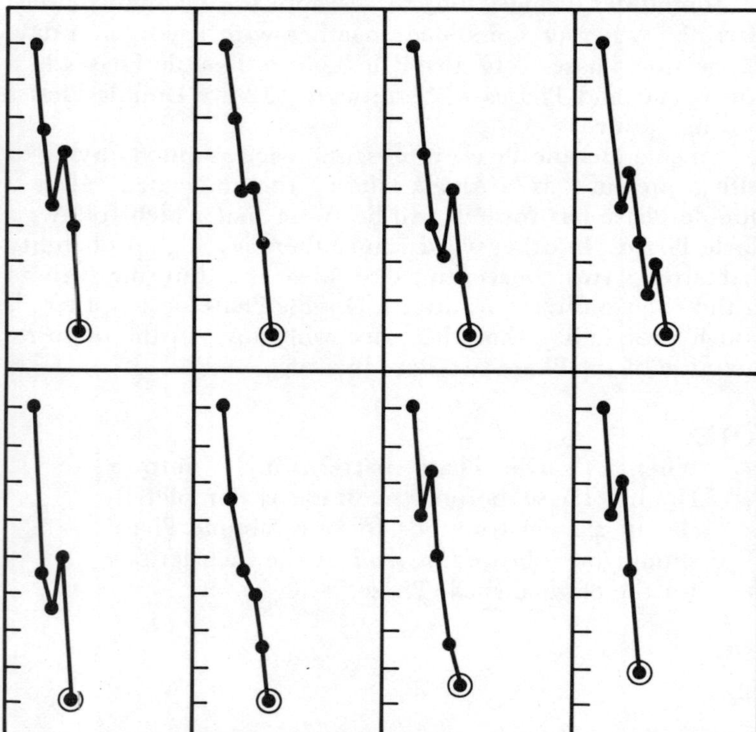

NO. 21 NO. 22 NO. 23 NO. 24

DOUBLE CONGESTION PHASES
#25 thru #32
Uptrend

For an existing LONG position: Take profit or cover position by *selling* at the top of the Phase.

To scalp: Sell at the top of the Phase; then *buy* on the close of a second consecutive day down.

NO. 25 **NO. 26** **NO. 27** **NO. 28**

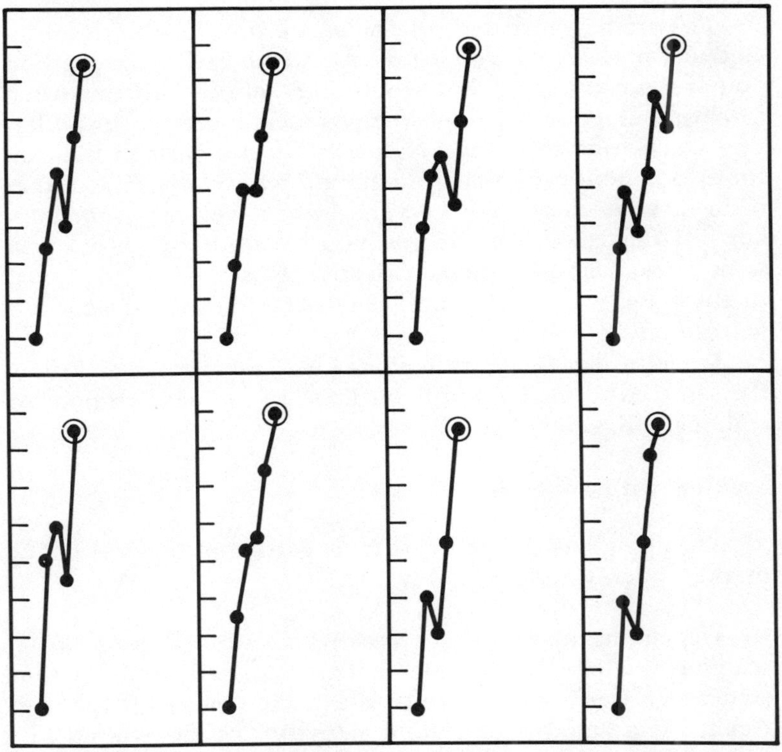

NO. 29 **NO. 30** **NO. 31** **NO. 32**

Profit-Taking With Congestion Phases

At the top of each page of Congestion Phases are two separate trading instructions. For the downtrend Phases the instructions are for an existing short position and for uptrend Phases the instructions are for an existing long position. This means that if you are already in the market and wish to take your profit, when a current pattern in your chart matches one of the Congestion Phases, follow the instructions to get out of the market. If you already have a loss and want to get out, the same instructions will minimize your additional loss.

The trading instructions for an existing position are included for those of you who are satisfied with the method you are already using, but would like help in knowing when to close out your position. Many traders loose profits by letting trades ride too long. Naturally, if you wish to hold on for a long period of time you should ignore any Phases that form in your chart until you are ready to get out of the market. It may also happen that you have initiated a position with one Phase and then inadvertently stayed in too long. In this case, simply wait until the instructions for the current pattern say "get out."

When using Congestion Phases for profit-taking, follow the same step-by-step points outlined in the next section for scalping with Congestion Phases.

Scalping with Congestion Phases

"Scalping" as defined earlier, is getting in and out of the market quickly and profitably.

Depending upon the patterns which form in your chart, scalping can be a continuous activity of two, three or four trades per week, or may only allow one complete trade per week. The amount of trading activity you do will also be dependent upon the extent of your finances; if you are able to initiate a trade every time a Phase pattern shows up in your chart, you will be trading more often than if you can trade with only one contract at a time.

The principle behind Congestion Phases is that the pressure of buying and selling, or rally and reaction, discussed in Chapter 3, means that after a two consecutive day move, there is about a 75% probability that on the third day the price will reverse it's direction. If this does not happen, the price has moved in the same direction for three consecutive days and there is now a 75% probability that the price will reverse on the third day. Again, if it does not, a double Phase has formed meaning that there now exists a 75% probability that the price will immediately reverse for two consecutive days.

In order to describe how to trade with Congestion Phases, I will take you step by step through a chart of May, 1975 corn closing prices from March 3 to April 24. This time period contains two congestion periods. I will include as much detail as possible. The point at which each trade is initiated is labelled by a letter of the alphabet for your convenience in locating them in the chart.

The first congestion period is verified on March 14 at $2.83.

On March 14, Phase #3 has formed. You BUY at the bottom of the Phase (A). Since the trading action must take place immediately after verifying that a Congestion Phase has formed, your orders must be placed within the last ten, or less, minutes of the trading day. If you are watching the prices or call your broker for them, you will know with reasonable certainty that the price is going to close either higher or lower than the previous day.

In the case of trade "A" in the May '75 Corn chart, during the last ten minutes of the trading day, you would have told your broker to place a market order to "buy on the close." Some traders or brokers may dispute the effi-

Figure 6

CORN, May 1975

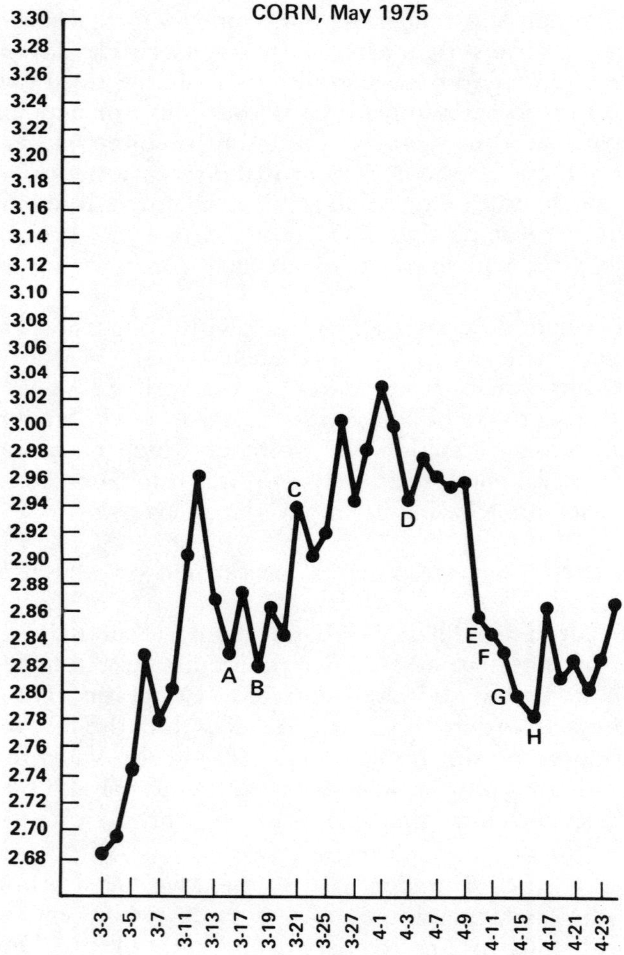

ciency of this "close call" type of order placing, but, I, and others using the Congestion Phase System, have placed orders in this manner successfully for years. On rare occasions it does happen that your order is not filled. If this happens, put your order in to buy (or sell) on the open the next trading day. It is sometimes riskier to trade the next morning because the price may change, but usually it opens close enough to the closing price to still be valid.

Now that we are long with a contract of May '75 corn on March 14, we must look for the price to close higher than the $2.83 price we paid in order to sell the contract. This happens on the next trading day, March 13. At the end of the trading day on March 13, you would have known that the price would close higher than $2.83 so we placed an order with our broker to "sell on the close." Your profit would have been $225, since we sold it at $2.87½.

As you continue to look for Congestion Phase patterns, March 18 reveals Congestion Phase pattern #21, a double Phase forms in the chart, (trade B). The trading instructions for this double Phase say to wait for two consecutive days up to sell because there is a high probability that this will happen. However, the price closes higher the first day but lower on the second day. At this point, if you wish to sell because the price failed to close higher on the second day after the Phase formed, you may do so and take the small amount of profit, $125. If you elected to hold on another day to see what would happen, you would have had a greater profit. In this case it would be a low-risk move to hold on because there is not a two consecutive day move up that would indicate the price would close lower the next day, and there is probably enough reaction pressure from the previous double phase to force the price higher the next day.

On March 21 the price hit $2.94 creating Phase #13, (trade C). You sell a contract at $2.94 and then buy a contract on March 24, for a profit of $175.

The price breaks through the congestion top on March 25.

On April 3 (D) the price has closed two consecutive days lower than a new high price in our chart, so we have confirmed a new top boundary of the congestion period. We can now BUY a contract at the close of the second consecutive day down. This is Phase #6 (trade D) and sell it on the next day's higher close of $2.97 for a $150 profit.

We continue to plot and on April 11, the price has closed lower for two consecutive days (two ½-cent-day moves are counted as one) and we BUY a contract (E) at $2.84¼. On the next trading day, April 14, the price closes down a third day, so we BUY another contract according to the instructions for Phase #4 which has formed, (trade F). On April 15 the price closes lower for a fourth day creating Phase #18, a double Phase pattern, (trade G) and on April 16 the price closes lower again for the fifth day (H), Phase #22, also a double Phase. The price reverses on April 17, but then closes lower on April 18.

Since we are looking for a second consecutive day on which to sell our contracts, instead of selling here because the price failed to immediately close higher two days in a row, we have the choice of waiting to see if the price will close higher for two consecutive days in the near future. The trading instructions say to wait for a second day up to sell and this may not happen immediately, although it usually does.

If you are able to wait four more trading days, the price does close two consecutive days up and if you sold your four contracts on April 24, you would have a net profit from these four contracts of $1,025.

Maximizing Profit at a Key Time

Although nice profits can be accrued while trading in only one contract with the Congestion Phase System, an obvious way of increasing profits is to trade in multiple contracts when initiating trades.

Another way to increase profits with this system is to buy one or more additional contracts at a key time while holding a long position, or selling additional contracts at a key time when having a short position. Certain congestion phase patterns signal the most advantageous time to add contracts. At such a time, the basic trading rules may be replaced by a variation. Following is a variation I have labelled "A." It is for a three consecutive day move.

Variation A

> When a commodity's price (in a congestion period) goes either up or down three consecutive days, and contracts have been bought/sold on both the second and third consecutive days, sell/buy the two-day phase contract(s) on the next higher day's close. Then, before the opening of the next trading day, place a stop-loss order just below/above the previous day's closing price* and sell/buy the remaining contract(s) at the close of that day.

The underlying principle of the Congestion Phase System is the natural pressure of buying and selling in the marketplace. This is discussed in detail in the next chapter. As each congestion phase forms, there is a 75 percent probability that trading pressure will force the price in the opposite direction of the phase's pressure.

The Variation A principle is that since three days up or down affords more pressure than two days up or down, the chances are greater that the subsequent reaction will be more than a one-day move. Placing a stop order will protect profit already accrued. The increased odds in this instance make it a key time to maximize profit by taking advantage of it whenever it appears in one's chart.

*10 points for live cattle and pork bellies and 1 cent for grains. In turbulent markets, such as gold or silver, place stops in amounts at your discretion.

Using Stop-Loss Orders with the Congestion Phase System

Placing "stops" has always been a common and necessary tool in limiting losses. With the Congestion Phase System, you need to place a Stop Loss order only when the price is near a high or low boundary of a current congestion period, and a breakthrough would bring loss; or when using the Variation A procedure.

Naturally if you are long near the top of the congestion or short close to the bottom of a congestion, you may wish to hold on to your contract(s) since a strong move is indicated. You may, of course place stops within the congestion period if you feel so inclined.

Profit Potential

To illustrate the profit potential of trading with Congestion Phases, following are records of trades I made in December, 1979 Live Cattle, February, 1979 Pork Bellies and December, 1979 Wheat. The tables of trading records are self-explanatory, and each congestion phase is coded with a letter of the alphabet in the chart.

I will, however, go step by step through trade #5 (June 29 to July 5) of the December, 1979 Live Cattle chart (Fig. 7), to further explain the use of the Variation X principle.

On the close of live cattle on June 29, I bought one contract per the trading rule for Phase #3 (E in chart). On the next trading day, July 2, the price closed lower for the third day in a row, Phase #4 (F), so I bought another contract as Phase #4 dictates. According to the standard trading rule for both Phases 3 and 4, both should be sold on the next higher day's closing price, which was July 3. This would have brought a profit of $628. However, I opted to use the Variation, and sold only one contract at the close of trading on July 3. Then, on the opening of the market the next trading day, July 5 (July 4 was a holiday), I put in a stop-loss order at 67.72 on the remaining contract, which is 10 points below the previous day's close of 67.82. When, by the end of the day, July 5, it was apparent that the price would close higher, I put in my order to sell the remaining contract on the close. I thus realized a profit from this strategy of $1,040 ($4 a point); $412 more than if I had stayed with the basic trading rules for phases 3 and 4.

The Congestion Phase System In Brief

- Determine whether or not your commodity is currently in a period of market congestion.
- Familiarize yourself with all the Congestion Phases and Double Congestion Phases.
- When a Congestion Phase pattern forms in your chart, follow the trading instructions for that Phase.
- Place orders at the market price "on the close" after checking the price ten, or less, minutes before the close of the trading day.
- When one Congestion Phase patterns becomes part of another Phase before you have closed out your position, trade according to the new Phase's instructions.
- Always use a Stop-Loss order when the price is near either of the limits of the congestion period and you are not in an advantageous position if it should break through.
- Continually make trades whenever a Congestion Phase forms in your chart.
- As soon as the current congestion is broken through, do not trade until you have verified a new congestion period.

Figure 7

LIVE CATTLE, December 1979

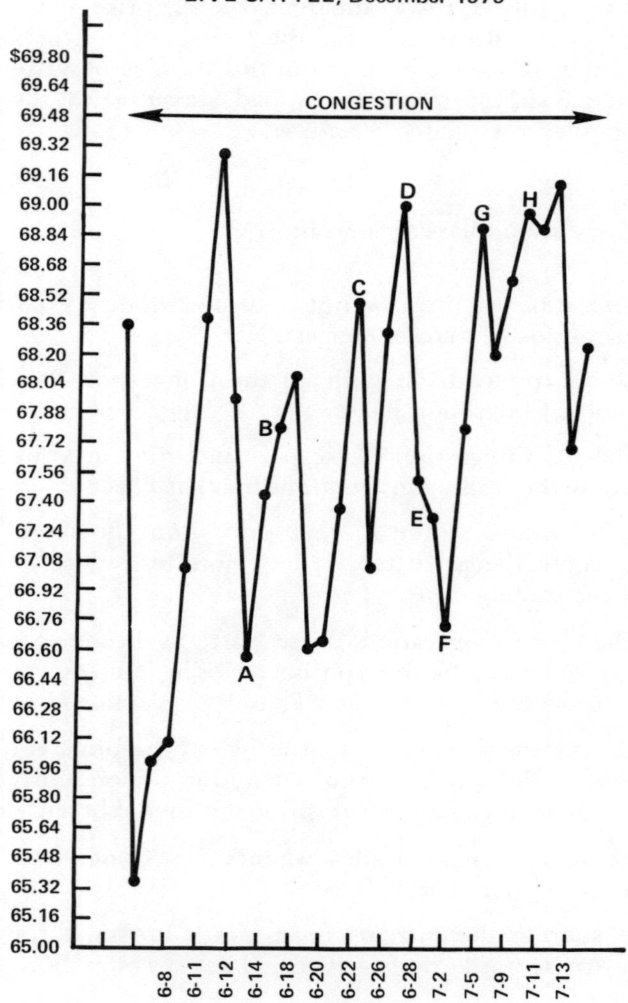

Table 1

TRADING RECORD OF DECEMBER, 1979 LIVE CATTLE USING CONGESTION PHASES

(*denotes the completion of a trade)

Trade No.	Date	Price (Points)	Coded on chart as	Phase No.	Trading Action	Profit/ Loss
1.	6/13	66.45	A	3	buy	
	6/14	67.45			sell*	$ 400
2.	6/15	67.80	B	10	sell	
	6/18	68.10		12	sell	
	6/19	66.60			buy*	1,080
3.	6/22	68.50	C	11	sell	
	6/25	67.05			buy*	580
4.	6/27	69.00	D	11	sell	
	6/28	67.50			buy*	600
5.	6/29	67.32	E	3	buy	
	7/2	66.75	F	4	buy	
	7/3	67.82		Var. A	sell*	200
	7/5	68.85		Var. A	sell*	840
6.	7/5	68.85	G	11	sell	
	7/6	68.20			buy*	260
7.	7/10	68.97	H	11	sell	
	7/11	68.85			buy*	48
			GROSS PROFIT			$4,008

Figure 8

PORK BELLIES, February 1979

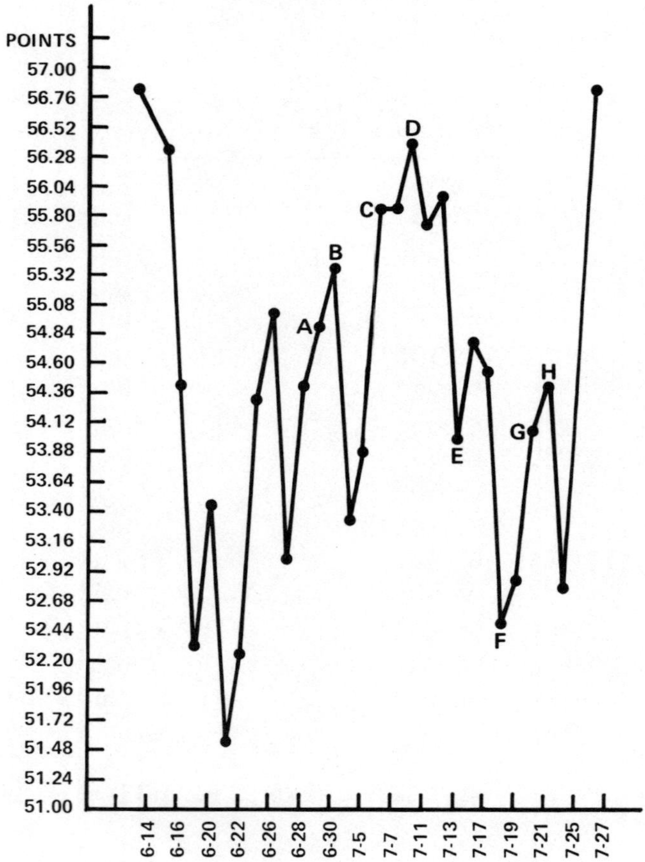

Table 2

TRADING RECORD OF FEBRUARY, 1979 PORK BELLIES USING CONGESTION PHASES

(*denotes the completion of a trade)

Trade No.	Date	Price (Points)	Coded on chart as	Phase No.	Trading Action	Profit/ Loss
1.	6/29/78	54.92	A	11	sell	
	6/30	55.40	B	12	sell	
	7/3	53.85		Var. A	buy*	$ 407
	7/5	53.95	"buy" stop executed*			551
2.	7/5	55.90	C	14	sell	
	7/10	56.40	D	12	sell	
	7/11	55.75		Var. A	buy*	57
	7/12	55.85	"buy" stop executed*			209
3.	7/13	54.00	E	5	buy	
	7/14	54.77			sell*	293
4.	7/18	52.50	F	6	buy	
	7/19	52.85			sell*	133
5.	7/20	54.07	G	14	sell	
	7/21	54.37	H	12	sell	
	7/24	52.50		Var. A	buy*	597
	7/25	52.60	"buy" stop executed*			674
			GROSS PROFIT			$2,921

Figure 9
WHEAT, December 1979

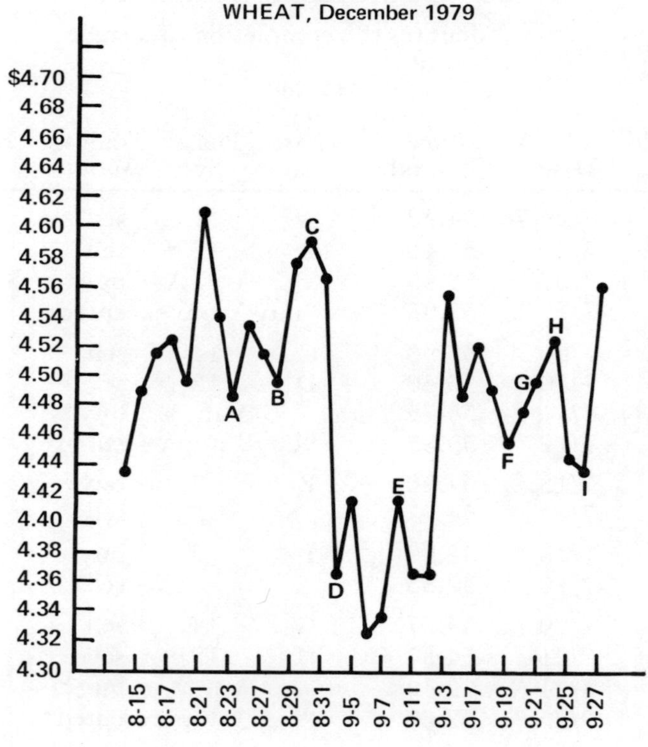

Table 3

TRADING RECORD OF DECEMBER, 1979 WHEAT USING CONGESTION PHASES

(*denotes the completion of a trade)

Trade No.	Date	Price (Points)	Coded on chart as	Phase No.	Trading Action	Profit/ Loss
1.	8/23	4.48½	A	3	buy	
	8/24	4.53½			sell*	$ 250
2.	8/28	4.49½	B	3	buy	
	8/29	4.57¾			sell*	425
3.	8/30	4.59	C	10	sell	
	8/31	4.56¼			buy*	140
4.	9/4	4.36¼	D	6	buy	
	9/5	4.41½			sell*	263
5.	9/10	4.41½	E	14	sell	
	9/11	4.36¾			buy*	240
6.	9/19	4.45½	F	3	buy	
	9/20	4.47½			sell*	100
7.	9/21	4.49¼	G	11	sell	
	9/24	4.52¾	H	12	sell	
	9/25	4.44½		Var. A	buy*	240
	9/26	4.43¾		Var. A	buy*	450
8.	9/26	4.43¾	I	2	buy	
	9/27	4.56			sell*	613
				GROSS PROFIT		$2,721

Commodity markets and their fluctuations cannot be fitted into an exact science. It is important to realize that the Congestion Phase system is not a science, but rather a tool to use to increase consistently successful commodity trading. The trading instructions and "rules" are based on rates of probability and do not pretend to be exact or without exception. The significance of using Congestion Phases is so that you will be putting the odds in your favor. I think you may agree that that is quite a lot.

WHY THE CONGESTION PHASE SYSTEM WORKS

There are natural laws, or principles, which govern price activity in the marketplace. Although there are many complex factors which affect the market, there are, in reality, only a few basic principles of price movement. In other words, the causes of price fluctuations are merely incidental to the movements themselves. If a trader can discover the underlying principles of why the market does what it does, he can then proceed to trade in rhythm with the market instead of trading according to what he "thinks" the market will do.

The only thing we really can "know" about prices is this: they fluctuate. You may think this statement is so simple that it is inane. But the truth is often so simple we reject it, relentlessly searching for a more complicated explanation.

The simplicity of natural laws governing the market is indeed one of the more fascinating aspects of the commodity futures game. I will now enumerate these principles. These principles are what the Congestion Phase System is made of, as well as an explanation of how the market works.

The Principle of Rally and Reaction

Prices are forced up (rally) and down (reaction) by the natural buying and selling in the market. On a day-to-day basis, buying and selling have a cause-effect relationship, each day to the previous day. If a commodity's price has gone up yesterday, some traders who are long will take their profit today, and other traders will take a short position, causing a reaction when there is more selling than buying.

There is a rally-reaction phenomenon which occurs repeatedly in periods of market congestion. It is: *two consecutive days of rally are followed by a day of reaction* and *two consecutive days of reaction are followed by one day of rally*. This can be explained in terms of "pressure." The pressure of two days dominated by buying cause the third day to be dominated by selling, and vica versa.

This phenomenon is the basic Congestion Phase and can be stated as "two days up, one down" and "two days down, one up." Other congestion phases build upon this basic unit, and occur in periods of congestion about 75% of the time.

The Principle of Market Congestion

Market Congestion can be characterized as a natural tug-of-war between the "bears" and the "bulls." These opposing forces equalize, or suppress, the tendency of extreme stretches of price movement either high or low, for a limited time.

Congestion periods can last from one week to several months. Some years have had long stretches of congestion periods in most markets, other years have shorter congestion periods.

Since market congestion is predictable, trading in these periods with a system that is based on its characteristic patterns can be said to be reasonable "safer" than other times when the market has not stabilized into this median range.

Fundamental Influences

Commodity traders who follow fundamental analysis, incorporate their "opinions" based on the "data" they study into their trading decisions. Daily prices reflect both fundamental and technical philosophies in this way. In other words, the fluctuations of prices confirm the opinions of thousands of traders, based on their own thinking and study. The Congestion Phase trader, therefore, is relieved of the mental calculations, guesswork and worry by the other traders in the market.

The Random-Walk Theory

According to the random-walk theory of price movement, in highly competitive, organized markets, price changes will be so close to random as to be virtually indistinguishable from random.

This theory contradicts both fundamental and technical approaches to market analysis. There is a great deal of evidence to support the conclusion that if several random walks were plotted on the same graphs as stock or commodity prices, you could not distinguish which was which.

Academic types have made elaborate statistical tests with computers and have found that it is not unreasonable to think of market prices as random walks.

Although most of the examination of this theory by statisticians and economists have been directed to the securities market rather than commodities, if you wish to read more about this theory, there are several books on the market that deal with it.

I mention this theory here because I feel it ties in with the principles I have discussed previously. There is growing evidence that there exist underlying, mathematic or statistical probability patterns, that cannot be explained in any other way than to say they are "laws." The "why" of these laws are into a whole other realm of life, and I leave it to you to explore the reasons if you so desire. I may be curious why a television works, but I am satisfied to simply use it, thus proving that it does work.

BASIC METHODS OF COMMODITIES MARKET ANALYSIS AND HOW THEY COMPARE TO THE CONGESTION PHASE SYSTEM

Commodities speculators use one or a combination of three basic methods to analyze and predict the behavior of commodity prices: fundamental, mechanical and technical.

The Fundamental Method

The fundamental method uses supply and demand factors as its basis. A trader using this approach relies on Department of Agriculture data, crop reports, exports, weather forecasts, government loan rates, seasonal trends in prices, inflation and deflationary forces, etc.

Through the accummulation of this type of data, the fundamentalist tries to estimate what the supply will be and weights this estimate against what he determines the demand for the commodity will be.

In reality, however, what may seem like "data" about supply and demand, can sometimes be merely *rumor*. It is not uncommon for government reports to be reversed in a matter of weeks or even days. Sometimes unconfirmed or partial information is circulated as fact. In addition, the market often goes completely contrary to fundamental considerations due to technical or other factors.

A fundamental trader is interested in long-range movements and must be prepared to wait it out.

Supply and demand factors are so numerous and complicated that it is a mind-boggling task to keep track of them, as illustrated in the following chart:

The simplicity of trading with the Congestion Phase system over the fundamental analysis method is obvious. Fundamentalists may deny it, but there are just too many external factors to take into account. Actually, the natural response of the market to fundamental influences is reflected in the day by day price fluctuations, so there is no need to seek them out for analysis.

The Mechanical Method

A mechanical trading method is one which uses rigid trading rules to be followed faithfully by the trader. They are usually based on some mathematical formula as a means of predicting the "right time" to trade. A sample mechanical method which is based on seasonal price changes is the well-known "The Voice From the Tomb."

This technique is said to have been willed to the heirs of a wealthy speculator many years ago, and is based on traditional harvest days, the affect of which have been greatly eliminated by complex governmental regulations in today's market.

"The Voice From the Tomb"

WHEAT		CORN	
Buy	*Sell*	*Buy*	*Sell*
February 22	January 10	March 1	May 20
July 1	May 20	June 25	August 10
November 28	September 10		

Figure 10

THE DEMAND AND SUPPLY STRUCTURE FOR PORK

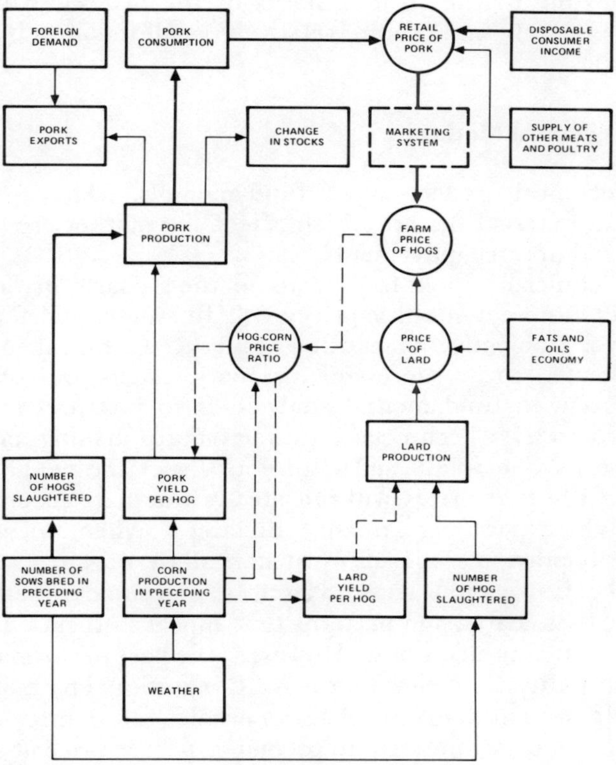

Arrows show direction of influence. Heavy arrows indicate major paths of influence which account for the bulk of the variations in current prices. Light solid arrows indicate definite but less important paths. Dashed arrows indicate paths of negligible, doubtful, or occasional importance.

U.S. Dept. of Agriculture Neg. 48936-X Bureau of Agricultural Economics

I've known traders who have followed "The Voice" and claim they have made more profitable trades than not, but this is a waiting game and requires large outlays of capital.

The Congestion Phase system, in comparison, is not rigid, but flexible to the current status of the market, will yield profits quickly and require relatively small financial backing.

The Technical Method

Technical traders avoid fundamentals. They presume that all external factors which affect the market are already reflected in price movements.

Technicians look for trends in their charts in order to predict how commodity prices will fluctuate, and feel they are more objective than other traders. Technical methods are claimed to be successful for many traders, but the trick here, as with fundamental analysis, is to interpret information correctly. Technicians are famous for making spectacular profits one week, and enormous losses the next. It is a fact of life that prices will not always fluctuate according to what their past performance dictates. When unexpected moves happen, technicians must start all over again.

The Congestion Phase System is a technical method in that it uses charts, and patterns that appear in them on which to base trading decisions. However, the past performance of a commodity is irrelevant to the Congestion Phase System, and my system does not claim to predict future price moves. It is, in fact, not possible to predict a specific price at a given time. The Congestion Phase System is more realistic in that it is based on what is happening today.

The Congestion Phase chart is simpler than any technician's chart because it plots only closing prices, which are a summary of each day's price movement.

Rather than being concerned with specific prices, the Congestion Phase System looks for the pattern of fluctuation only. The effectiveness of the system can be credited to this fact. We know for sure that prices will fluctuate, but not how much. If we have bought a contract we wish only to sell it higher to make a profit.

Other Advantages of the Congestion Phase System

Because you trade only in congestion periods with the Congestion Phase system, you are protected from large losses brought about by getting caught in a straight-away move. No other method can provide the same type of protection.

A universal problem, admitted to by both professional and novice commodity traders, is knowing when to get in and out of the market. No matter how tried and true a trader feels his method is, the decision of exactly when to buy and sell usually boils down to agonizing guesswork. The congestion Phase System solves this problem by telling you when you have the best chance of making a profitable trade.

The advantage of trading with The Congestion Phase System is that you will enjoy a higher percentage of reliability. Profits may not be as large as those gained through another method, but the beauty of Congestion Phases is that they can also be used with other systems to enhance a trader's chances of success.

The famous advice of "cut your losses short and let your profits run" is obviously good, but the question arises, "how?" How do you know when it is too soon to take profit or the right time to take a small profit. This advice is like telling someone to "stay happy and healthy." It sounds good and everybody would like to do it, but the crucial question of "how" goes unanswered. Probably the same number of people who are able to follow the latter advice, can follow the former.

THE PERSONAL CHARACTERISTICS OF A SUCCESSFUL TRADER

A U.S. Department of Agriculture survey of 8,783 commodities speculators reported: "In general, the chances for success in grain futures trading did not differ greatly from one occupation to another. Special knowledge of the commodity traded seemed to have little effect on the outcome of speculative trading during the period studied . . . There is no evidence that the largest size (big money) classes include a higher proportion of successful traders than the group with smaller average positions."

In the Conclusion of the best-selling *Playboy's Investment Guide* this statement appears:

". . . the fact is that most of the people who have amassed great speculative wealth in contemporary America – those who have created fortunes rather than inheriting them – are not, as a rule, terribly intelligent, terribly well-educated or even terribly hard workers. There are exceptions, of course. But not many. And most of these are intelligent enough to admit that brains, knowledge and dilligence had precious little to do with their speculative success.

. . . What do they have in common? . . . psychological self-mastery.

. . . Above all, successful speculation requires not knowledge, nor training nor some unique insight into human affairs, but simply self-awareness. You must know your strengths, appreciate your weaknesses and mercilessly throttle the temptation to lie to yourself."

Since any system of trading must be put into play by a human being, to a large extent, its effectiveness is dependent upon the degree to which it is followed. Of course, the more complicated a system, the most difficult it is to follow. This difficulty is compounded by the reality of human weakness.

I feel that this area of human nature is an important one to examine in relationship to our success as a commodities trader.

Psychological studies have shown that pressures, tensions, anxieties and fear seriously impair decision-making skill. The market and the trader are an interacting unit which makes up the trading system. The market affects the trader emotionally. If the trader can become sensitive to the market's affect on him, he can more effectively apply his method.

William Morris, author of *How to Get Rich Slowly, But Almost Surely*, published by Reston Publishing Co., Reston, Virginia, suggests that self-perception and self-awareness through researching one's own attitudes and emotions " . . . may be the real secret of consistent financial effectiveness. It may be the essential prerequisite to getting rich . . . It is almost surely the key to understanding why most people do not get rich at all."

Mr. Morris advises that an investor probe his inner feelings in order to determine the market's influence on him. A few of the questions he suggests we ask ourselves are:

"How do you feel when you've experienced a sudden large loss or large gain? Does the emotional impact show up in the way you deal with your job, your family, or the next financial decision you make? Does it affect your attitude towards your family budget? Toward taking your spouse out for dinner? Toward the kids' next request?

Are the funds you're using all you have on which to retire, educate the children, or meet a major emergency? Does the fear and tension associated from the possibility of wiping out your financial future bring you to a high state of nervousness or panic when the market drops sharply?

Are you holding some things that went down a long time ago and stayed there, hoping that one of these days you'll be able to get even and get out?

Are you losing sleep over your financial operations? Are you a worrier? Do you call your broker frequently and read everything you can get your hands on, searching for fragments which tend to confirm your judgment and restore a little of your confidence?

Do you feel that you should be in the market all the time? Can you stay out for awhile, or are you too afraid of missing a rise?

Do you get upset by the stories of people who have made a killing?

Does it seem that there are so many different kinds of opportunities available that you can hardly decide what to do? Do you often jump out of a recent commitment because something that seems better comes to your attention?"

Your self-examination may lead you to the realization that you sometimes act in a self-defeating way. Perhaps you tend to be greedy, are over-eager to succeed, or rush too quickly into some risky speculative scheme. You may hang on too long to a losing position or change commitments too often. You may have discovered that you are easily discouraged, or overly encouraged by market activity.

Whatever it is you are discovering about yourself in these areas, what every trader needs to do is insulate himself or herself from all psychological pressure. Since these psychological facts are often unconscious, they need to be brought out in the open. Once they are uncovered and recognized, controlling them becomes a much easier task.

Three professional speculators were interviewed by *Commodities* magazine for their September, 1972 issue. I have included some passages here to illustrate how these men have learned to curb the personality traits they deem a hindrance to their success:

Daniel Kelly:

"It is very easy to fall in love with a position. . . I have to fight it all the time. I had recently been rather friendly to the oil market, and it had been breaking and breaking and breaking. About a week ago it was just so dismal you absolutely had to go short. But I knew it would be wrong, so I went up to my office for an hour just so I wouldn't sell. . . The big tmptation is to say that it's never going to stop going down. But this is a futures market, and it was adjusting to factors which several people, including myself, had not been perceptive enough to understand.

I have always contended that I don't have the disposition to be in the business myself. I worry. Things bother me. . . . I'm very conservative, cautious. I try to treat this as a business just like any other business.

Gerald Hatoff, classifying himself as a technician, had the following to say:

"Equally important (to the trading method) are the psychological factors that each trader or speculator must face up to. He has to know himself. Children, when they are 'bad,' are punished by their parents in the hope that this unpleasantness will deter any repetition of the behavior. A trader or speculator who has sustained a loss must be on guard that the unpleasantness of the loss does not deter him from entering into what may be profitable subsequent trade.

". . . There is a euphoric feeling when the market is going with you. I think that all speculators should really have an accounting with themselves each night, based on settlement prices.

Paul McGuire who characterizes himself as an "eclectic... and perhaps a cynic" offers the following views:

"Even when an opinion is downright silly, if it is held by enough people it will affect the market."

". . . I lost on a modest 'side-play in silver, where I had no strong conviction, no basis for precise analysis, but simply got involved in the action. Such careless trading is a temptation even veteran traders find hard to resist. In the long run, profits accrue only from careful analysis calculated and avoiding the "opportunities" which beckon but have no real substance.

These three professionals exhibit similar traits regardless of their diverse trading techniques and styles. They are all confident, fight their weaknesses and know themselves well. They have a common-sense, methodical approach to their trading and avoid "gambling," or going after an ephemeral rainbow in the sky. They are not afraid to admit they make mistakes, but they recover immediately with a positive determination to succeed the next day.

A Merrill Lynch booklet, designed for a quick quiz on grading your potential as a commodities speculator asks the following questions:

– Are you an agressive, active investor – psychologically attuned to go after sizeable capital gains in a fast-moving market?

– Are you temperamentally able to evaluate – and accept – substantial risk in the pursuit of extraordinary gains?

– Are you able to form a basic trading plan – and stick to it – even during a temporary bad streak when everything seems to turn sour?

– Do you, in some measure, have a cool, analytic mind? Can you resist mob psychology;

– Do you have the courage to act promptly on decisions once they're made? (This may not be as easy as it sounds-when it's your own money, and the risks are by no means negligible.)

A theory of "risk-aversion," developed through ten years of research and experience of Dr. Jack J. Hayden, offers a unique explanation of why only a few investors make money in speculative markets and most do not.

Dr. Hayden believes that all investors fall into a range of optimists and pessimists, and their behabior is coupled with a degree of "risk-aversion" inherent in their personalities. An optimist is more comfortable with a "long" position and a pessimist with a "short" position.

His studies have found that individuals who are optimistic and at the same time have a high degree of "risk-aversion" react more emotionally when making trade decisions than does anyone else. This group tends to be the least successful in speculative markets. This group also engulfs the vast majority of investors.

According to this theory, people who have a low aversion to risk, whether optimistic or pessimistic, have the best chance of making profits on their speculative investments.

If we incorporate this idea into others mentioned in this Chapter, it adds more support to the contention that the trader must know himself and discover what characteristics he should take measures against, and also points up the fact that emotions are the enemy of the commodities trader – especially fear.

Mental Attitude

Perhaps this whole chapter boils down to having the correct mental attitude. For it is our minds, after all, that provide objectivity and control.

Make a determined effort to follow through with your decisions. Remind yourself of the points brought out in this Chapter, and re-read these pages from time to time.

Train yourself to recognize your emotional impulses and their significance. Remind yourself to evaluate how you feel at the time you make a decision.

Through self-mastery then, you will be able to follow a system's rules much more effectively. If the system you are using is based on sound market principles, and is reliable – namely the Congestion Phase System, you can confidently proceed with becoming an outstanding success.

HOW TO PROTECT YOURSELF FROM YOUR BROKER

The Case for Skepticism

During the long siege of the stock market in 1969-1970 many stock brokers turned to commodities markets as a means of survival. Although most of these brokers knew little or nothing about trading in futures, they began filling orders and dispensing the advice they read in the media, advisory services or simply "reliable" hearsay within the company. To say that this is the blind leading the blind is hardly an overstatement. In addition, many brokers hired in recent years by brokerage firms are ex-commodity speculators who have lost a lot of money in the market. Some feel they were "unlucky' or didn't have enough capital to "hold out til the market turned around," or that they should have listened to their own intuition.

In the course of researching this book, I interviewed six commodity brokers in the Southern California area. I asked each one for the average life span of a commodities account. Three said the majority of their accounts lasted up to three

"Reprinted with Permission of COMMODITIES Magazine"

months. One said most lasted up to one year, with a few lasting two years or longer. The other two reported they had not yet had a commodities account open for more than one year!

It would be absurd to blame brokers entirely for their customers' losses, but the fact is that many traders listen to what their brokers have to say.

Although questioning six brokers is a very small sampling, the impressions and opinions I got from them coupled with the same from many brokers of my personal acquaintance over the years, I will summarize a generalization of what seem to be some prevalent attitudes among commodity brokers.

– Many brokers admit to having emotional biases towards their customers. If they do not "like" a customer, the broker tends to give him less attention and poorer service.

– Even when a customer does not want his advice, brokers often try to disuade the customer from making a trade the broker feels is wrong.

– Most brokers feel that the reason traders lose money in the market is because they act emotionally and do not understand how the markets work (the brokers think *they* do, however.)

– Most brokers are reluctant to take on female customers. If she is financially secure, emotionally stable and intelligent, a broker will probably take the account. Some brokerage houses refuse women's accounts altogether.

– A prevalent opinion among commodity brokers is that the U.S. Department of Agriculture falsifies crop reports and news releases in order to manipulate the market. To use the explanation by one broker I interviewed:

> The Department of Agriculture puts out a report that a certain number of bushels of wheat are under contract for export. If it is a very large amount, it causes the price to rise. Weeks later, the Department issues a revised report, saying that it had discovered an error in calculation or that the Department was given incorrect information which they based their figures on, and that a much lesser amount will be exported. While the price is high, the government sells wheat for the higher price.

Brokers say that about 75% of their customers listen to their advice, sometimes acting in agreement and sometimes not. They estimate that about 25% of their customers depend entirely upon their advice and trade according to it.

You Can Know More Than Your Broker

You may think that because a broker spends his days in a trading environment that he somehow assimilates information and "good tips" about the market. Actually, a broker's office is the worst place from which to evaluate market activity. Rumors flourish and emotions rein. News is often overemphasized and mis-interpreted.

Any trader is much better off to rely on his own charts. If you are using the Congestion Phase method to read your charts, you will know much more than your broker because the Congestion Phase System takes into account all market phenomenon, and outside influences. News and rumors and government reports are reflected in your chart and Congestion Phases will tell you how to act on the fluctuations to make money.

If your broker understands what is needed from him, he will function in a way that is beneficial to you – as one who fills your orders accurately and keeps you advised about your transactions.

How to Help Your Broker Help You

Tell your broker about how you will trade with Congestion Phases. Explain the basic principles, action and timing. Tell him that generally you will be placing orders at the close of the day. This will probably sound strange to him, since traders usually try to catch a specific price or move during the day. If he tries to advise you, ignore it.

Your broker will soon discover that you're on to something that works. He will probably start asking for *your* advice!

PART TWO

"IF YOU HAVE NEVER TRADED IN COMMODITY FUTURES BEFORE..."

WHAT COMMODITIES TRADING IS ALL ABOUT

Commodity futures markets were created because agricultural crops and goods are harvested in spring and fall but are needed throughout the year. Because commodity traders buy contracts consistently throughout the year they provide an even flow of availability of future contracts to buyers. This is an important function in keeping the market stable, or "liquid", as economists say. In other words, prices become more stable with a futures market, than if they were based exclusively on immediate supply and demand.

By providing stability to market prices, the trader relieves both the farmer and the processor of the risk involved in trying to establish a fair price for crops that are harvested at a future time. Processors, such as millers, have no way of knowing the condition or available quantity of the crop to be harvested months into the future, and farmers or growers have no guarantee of how much of their crop will be in demand or saleable. When they tried, a century ago, to barter between themselves, one of the parties would suffer severe loss when something unforeseen happened to the crop.

Figure 11

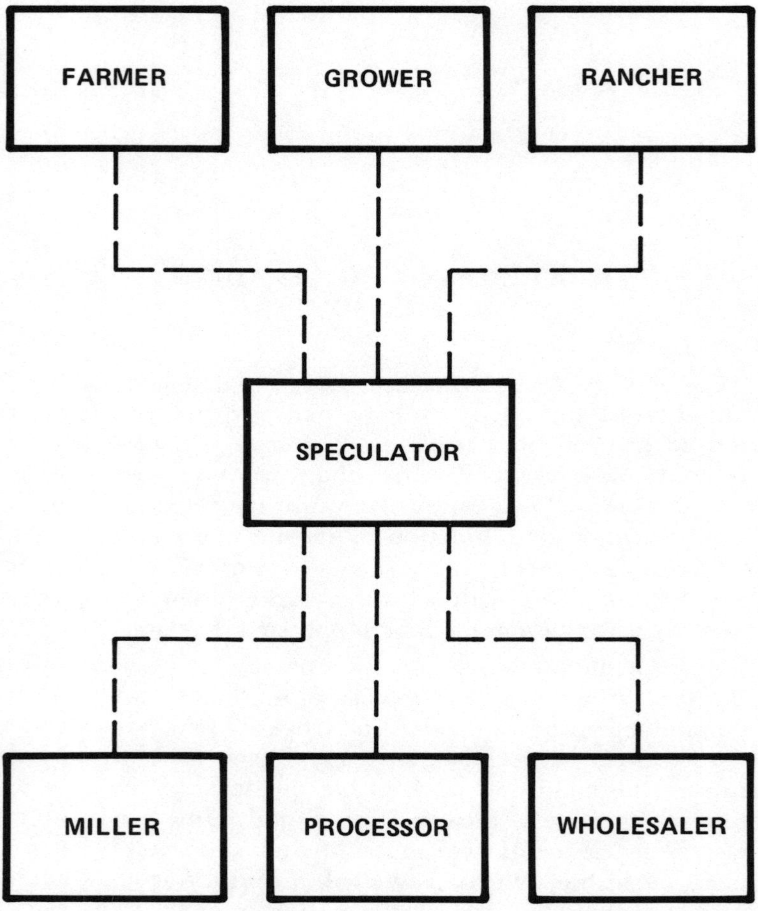
FARMER
GROWER
RANCHER
SPECULATOR
MILLER
PROCESSOR
WHOLESALER

The Speculator

The trader, or speculator, evolved from a few adventurous men who were willing to say, "I will assume the risk for both of you if I can make a profit on the difference between the price I pay and the price I get for completing the transaction." This arrangement has proven advantageous to all parties.

Commodities speculation is sometimes referred to as "gambling," but should not be confused with the artifically created type such as a casino. The risk involved with trading futures contracts is already inherent in our free enterprise economic system. Someone must assume the risks, whether it be the farmer, producer, miller or speculator. Since there are so many variables affecting commodity prices, i.e., production, processing, marketing, consumption, risk is unavoidable. The speculator is simply taking part in the risk in order to profit from changes in prices. He is contributing to the success of the entire economic process of cycling goods to consumers.

The Future Contract

A Future Contract is an agreement between two parties in which each agrees either to buy or to sell a specified amount of a commodity at a specified time in the future. In December, a trader may buy a contract in corn (buying a contract is called being "long") which will be harvested in September of the following year. Or, a trader can sell a contract of corn to a processor, promising to provide the specified commodity at a certain price when the crop is harvested (initiated a contract buy selling first is called taking a "short" position or being "short").

A contract may change hands hundreds of times before the contract matures at harvest time. Only 2% of the contracts initially bought and held until harvest. It is the parties who are the last holders of the contract who fulfill the promise to pay and deliver.

Future contracts are for standardized quantities. All grain contracts (wheat, corn, oats, soybeans) are for 5,000 bushels. A silver contract is for 5,000 ounces. A plywood contract is for 70,000 square feet.

Commodity Exchanges

Commodity exchanges are voluntary associations whose business is trading in futures contracts. Older exchanges were chartered by special legislative acts of the states in which they were located. More recent exchanges are organized under membership corporation laws.

Some of the major exchanges are the Chicago Board of Trade, the Kansas City Board of Trade, the Minneapolis Grain Exchange, the New York Mercantile Exchange and the Chicago Mercantile Exchange.

Some exchanges specialize, such as the New York Coffee & Sugar Exchange, the New York Cocoa Exchange and the New York Cotton Exchange.

There are over fifty commodities currently traded on there exchanges. Here is a partial listing:

Chicago Board of Trade

Corn
Wheat
Iced Broilers
Plywood
Silver
Soybeans
Soybean Oil
Soybean Meal
Gold
Oats

New York Mercantile Exchange

Potatoes
Platinum
Apples
Plywood

Chicago Mercantile Exchange
Live cattle
Fresh eggs
Live hogs
Frozen pork bellies

Following is a sample selection of contract sizes and commission rates:

COMMODITY	SIZE OF CONTRACT	COMMISSION PER CONTRACT*
Cattle (live)	40,000 lbs.	$50
Cocoa	30,000 lbs.	$70
Copper	50,000 lbs.	$56
Corn	5,000 bu.	$50+
Cotton (#2)	100 bales	$80
Eggs (Fresh)	18,000 doz.	$60
Hogs (live)	20,000 lbs.	$52
Lumber	40,000 bd. ft.	$55
Plywood	69,120 sq. ft.	$50+
Pork Bellies	30,000 lbs.	$55
Oats	5,000 bu.	$36+
Potatoes	45,000 lbs.	$30+
Soybeans	5,000 bu.	$55
Soybean Meal	100 ton	$50
Soybean Oil	60,000 lbs.	$50
Sugar	112,000 lbs.	$80+
Wheat	5,000 bu.	$55

*Approximate. Varies with brokerage firm.

The speed and excitement of trading on the floor of a commodity exchange is vividly described by Thomas A. Hieronymus in his observation of the Chicago Board of Trade in his textbook, *Economics of Futures Trading*, published by the Commodity Research Bureau, Inc., New York:

> "One need only stand on the visitor's balcony, watching the trading and the expressions

on the faces of the other visitors to gain a sense of mystery and confusion. The trading floor is . . . the size of a football field. On an ordinary day some six hundred people are present, a few are sitting at telephones but most are on their feet and in motion, some walking and some running. There are several dense concentrations of people standing on steps that form hexagonal pits. Here, the action is frantic with as many as 300 men shouting, waving their arms, and signaling with their fingers simultaneously. In isolation, as on a television camera , one trader bellows at the man next to him with such vigor that his face turns red, and waves both hands, a trading card, and a pencil in his face. The other reciprocates, both write quickly on cards, and turn to repeat the whole process to other traders or to the pit in general. A few feet away messengers run from telephones and other communications machines to the pits and back. Incongruously, there are other people similarly engaged or quietly watching, oblivious to the din surrounding them. High on the end wall there are huge electronic scoreboards with flashing numbers that seem to relate to a multiplicity of scores somehow ascertained from the action in the pits. But nothing is shown about which team has the ball. The visitor is told that the players do know what they are doing and the action somehow relates to the real world of commerce in grains, oilseeds, cattle and chickens."

Brokerage Firms

Brokerage firms, or commission houses, are intermediaries between the trading floor, or pit, and their customers. Customers are an assortment of individuals, commercial businesses, exporters or food processors.

Stock brokerage firms may have a few brokers who specialize in commodity market accounts, and some have a commodities "board" on which prices are continually revised during the trading day.

Commission houses, which deal exclusively in commodities market transactions can be found in most major cities. The larger firms hold memberships to most major exchanges.

The more commodities business a firm has, the better for the commodities customer in the way of service and attention.

A brokerage firm will require a minimum amount to open an account. This can vary from $1,500 to $5,000 or more. Some commission houses require only the amount of margin required for the specific future contract(s) you wish to trade in, to open an account.

Margin

"Margin" is a deposit required in order to initiate a position in the market. This acts as a guarantee that the parties to a contract will fulfill the terms of that contract. It is a "performance bond" held by the clearing-house.

Margin is relative to the price of the contract as well as the range of fluctuation permitted in that commodity in a day. The amount of margin, usually 5-10% of the value of the contract(s), may change according to market conditions. Sometimes margins are lowered to stimulate business. More transactions can take place if less capital is required to trade. When activity is vigorous and prices are climbing, margin is sometimes raised.

If the price of a contract fluctuates in a direction of loss, and the margin you have deposited will not cover the loss sufficiently, you will be asked to deposit more money to raise the level of protection on the contract.

For example, if the margin on a contract is 10¢ per bushel, and you wish to buy 2 contracts (10,000 bushels), you must deposit $1,000 on margin. If the price per bushel drops 5¢ after you buy it, you would get a "margin call" for $500 additional margin.

WHY TRADE IN COMMODITY FUTURES?

If you have investment funds you wish to multiply quickly, and in large proportions, commodities speculation is ideal for you. It is not unheard of for an initial capital investment in commodities to double or even to increase 1,000 percent. With the Congestion Phase system, you will be able to consistently make money, instead of the usual situation where a trader soon loses most, or all, of the profit he has recently made.

Many people hesitate to consider investing in commodity futures because of the high risk potential the market is reputed to have. But, if you follow the Congestion Phase system explained in this book, your investment mood, like mine, will be such that you'll think more in terms of profit than risk – because you will be taking more profits than risks!

Besides the big profits available in futures markets, there are many other advantages to commodity speculation.

More Action in Commodities

Many commodity traders are ex-securities investors who became bored with the relatively slow, long-range activities of stocks. Commodity prices change rapidly and fluctuate widely, providing much excitement along with a far greater opportunity to make money, sometimes on a daily basis.

Lower Capital Investment

Margin requirements for commodity trading are extremely low – five to ten percent of the purchase price. Margin requirements on stock purchases are around 65%. This means that if you have $3,000 in investment capital you could buy $5,000 worth of stock, or over $50,000 worth of commodities. This leverage is a big advantage for your capital to reap the highest gain.

Commissions are Lower

Commodity commissions are about one-eighth those on stocks, and cover both sides of the transaction (initiating and closing out a position), while stock commissions are charged on the buying and selling separately.

Commodities are Simpler

There are currently more than 1,500 different stocks and numerous other forms of investment. There are a little more than 50 commodities, falling within 25 basic product groups. Each commodity can be treated as a separate market in itself.

There is much less information needed to select a commodity to trade in. Most commodity brokers are familiar enough with the majority of them to give you adequate information.

Prices Are Contained by Trading Limits

Daily trading limits are set for the protection of traders. These limits prohibit prices from changing by more than a specified amount during any given daily trading session. For example, with a 10 cent trading limit on corn, the price can only fluctuate to 10 cents above or below the closing price of the previous day's session. These limits are adjusted periodically in relation to factors such as trading volume.

Daily trading limits protect commodity traders and brokers from the hysteria in the market which can cause irrational, drastic price swings. Trading limits allow for breathing time in which the market can regain normalcy.

Short Selling is Easy

Taking a short position in commodities is just as simple as taking a long position. A futures contract transaction is not an actual sale, but simply a promise to sell and deliver the commodity. When a trade is completed prior to the delivery day, no delivery is required. In a short sale of securities one must borrow the securities sold and ultimately return them to whom they were borrowed from.

Increasing Grain Exports

There is a growth trend in grain exports, due to increasing world demand. Today, one out of every four acres of grain planted is sent abroad. Wheat and soybean exports exceed this figure. Growing world markets mean an ever-increasing trading volume and overall rising prices in an already very active market.

Growing Interest in Commodities

Some brokerage firms have estimated a 25% annual increase in commodity transactions for each of the last three years. They predict this trend will continue to accelerate during the next decade.

As more people participate in commodity speculation, the increased activity stimulates price fluctuations. This creates a more active arena in which one can take advantage of healthy price movements.

The Chicago Mercantile Exchange estimates that the present 500,000 commodities futures traders will grow to 3 million by 1980 or sooner.

HOW TO FIND A "GOOD" COMMODITIES BROKER

A "good" broker is not one who goes to church on Sunday or participates in Boy Scout activities, but one concerned with how well he can execute your trading orders and take care of your account.

I have worked up some guidelines for interviewing a prospective (or existing) broker for evaluation:

1) ASK HIM HOW LONG HE HAS BEEN PLACING ORDERS IN COMMODITY MARKETS. If he's new at it, you'll probably be better off to look elsewhere. Experience (there are exceptions) is important in developing speedy and efficient service.
2) ASK HIM HOW MANY OF HIS EXISTING COMMODITY CUSTOMERS MAKE A TRADE ONCE A WEEK OR MORE. You want a broker who is filling orders on a regular basis, to assure that he is well-versed in procedure and problems that can come up.
3) ASK HOW FREQUENTLY HE CONTACTS A CUSTOMER WHO HAS A CURRENT POSITION. The answer to this should be "daily" or even "hourly." If he is devoting his attention to his customers, you can be pretty sure he will contact you quickly if need be.

4) ASK HOW MUCH OF HIS TOTAL COMMISSION IS FROM COMMODITIES ORDERS. If he says 50% or more you'll know that he's keenly interested in his commodity accounts. If he says less than half, his real interest is probably elsewhere, as well as his best service.

The following letter of woe appeared in the "Letters to the Editor" column of the *Commodity Journal*, published by the American Association of Commodity Traders:

"Gentleman:

. . . Several weeks ago, after trading with a firm dealing in commodity futures for some time, we gave our broker an order for wheat. At the time it was selling for $2.53 bu. We told him to buy it at $2.46 with a stop at $2.44.

About two days later the market dropped, and we heard via radio it was selling at $2.46 with a stop at $2.44.

About two days later the market dropped, and we heard via radio it was selling at $2.46 . . . then we heard it was $2.44. I did not call the broker as we had a definite understanding that he was to sell if the market dropped to $2.44. In fact when I placed the order he had repeated these figures several times.

Two days later he called to say he still had the wheat! As a result of this our loss ran in the neighborhood of $900.

Do we have any recourse? He simply did not place the stop loss and does not "recall" our giving him such a figure.

If we do not have any recourse what can one do to protect himself in placing orders by phone?"

The *Commodity Journal* Editor's reply was:

> "You have depicted one of the basic risks and dsyfunctions of the present loosely-structured system of placing orders by telephone. As we view it, you have little recourse, as it would

> simply be your word against the broker's. I would suggest that in the future you establish protection in one or both of two ways:
> 1)Confirm all your telephone instructions in writing and/or 2) ask your broker to mail you a confirmation of all advance "open" orders, including stop loss orders. Such a procedure would require just a few minutes on the part of either of you, and especially if you had a broker's confirmation establish your instructions on an undisputable basis."

The editor's advice is good, but the reason I have quoted the above letter is to point out the value of selecting a competent broker. If you read the customer's letter, with the aforementioned four questions to ask your broker in mind, you will discover how this victim of error could have saved himself from this situation by engaging a broker who contacts him daily (Point #3) and also by establishing his efficiency and his concern for his customers with the other questions.

The best relationship to have with your broker is one of mutual respect, with a clear cut identity of customer/broker.

HOW TO MAKE A CONGESTION PHASE CHART

A chart is a basic tool of a trader because it records price activity so that it can be studied and evaluated. All commodities traders use charts to some degree. If a trader does not keep his own charts, he studies those of a chart service, or relies on his broker, who studies charts.

If you have never made your own chart you can follow the step by step procedure in this chapter for making a simple chart which will give you all the information you need to trade successfully with the Congestion Phase system.

There are three things you will need to do before actually making the chart. They are:

1. *Assemble these materials*:

   a) 8½ X 11 graph paper, 4 or 6 squares to the inch.
   b) A 6-inch ruler or triangle (clear plastic is best).
   c) A sharp #2 (medium) pencil.
   d) Transparent tape.

2. *Choose a commodity to trade in*:

The decision of "which commodity" may depend upon

the amount of capital you have, but choose one which has a high volume of trading. Your broker can tell you which commodities are currently active. The month in which the crop is harvested is called the "delivery month." You will be trading in December oats, or July wheat, etc.

3. *Accumulate Price Data*:
Obtain the "closing prices" of your commodity from the ten trading days previous to the day you begin your chart. Commodity price quotations can be clipped from *The Wall Street Journal*, the *Journal of Commerce*, or any major city newspaper's financial section. You can find back issues at a library, or your broker can supply you with this data. Futures Prices are printed in these papers under columns headed "Open," "High," "Low" and "Close." It is the column headed "Close" that you will take the price from, across from name and delivery month of your commodity.

If there are two prices in the close column (split close), use the highest price. For example, in the following Futures Prices listing, the December Chicago-Wheat closing price is 3.80½-3.80. The price you would use in your chart is 3.80½.

Write the previous ten trading days' prices and dates on a piece of paper. Indicate which price is the highest of the group and which is the lowest.

Constructing the Chart

For the purpose of constructing a sample chart I will use July corn closing prices from January 17 through January 30, 1975.

Jan. 17 . . . . 3.21½
Jan. 20 . . . . 3.11½
Jan. 21 . . . . 3.16
Jan. 22 . . . . 3.05-3/4 (lowest)
Jan. 23 . . . . 3.15-3/4
Jan. 24 . . . . 3.22 (highest)

Futures Prices

Wednesday, March 26, 1975

COLUMN OF CLOSING PRICES

DECEMBER HIGH CLOSE IS 3.80½

	Open	High	Low	Close	Change	Season's High	Season's Low
CHICAGO – WHEAT							
May	373	382	369	378 376	+9½[illegible]	557	328½
July	362	368	358	367 366	+8¾to7¾	509	324½
Sept	368	373	365½	372	+7½	513	[illegible]
Dec	377	382	374½	380½ 380	+6½to6	523	[illegible]
Mar 76	383	386	380	386 385	+6to5	386	[illegible]
CORN							
May	294	301½	293½	300 300¼	+8to8¼	413	[illegible]
July	294½	301	293	300 301	+8½to9¼	411	[illegible]
Sept	287½	290¾	282	290½ 290¾	+9¾to10	388½	246¾
Dec	266½	274	266½	273¾ 273	+9to8½	355	234
Mar 76	271½	279½	271¾	279¾	+9¾	[illegible]	[illegible]
OATS							
May	146	151	145½	151	+6	[illegible]	[illegible]
July	140	145	140	145b	+6	[illegible]	[illegible]
Sept	138½	144	137½	144b	+6	[illegible]	[illegible]
Dec	141	145	141	145b	+6	[illegible]	[illegible]
SOYBEANS							
May	596	608¼	589½	608¼b	+20	971	487¾
July	593	609½	590	609½b	+20	972½	497½
Aug	595	610	590½	610b	+20	961	502
Sept	586	602	583	602	+18	945	498
Nov	577	594	574	594	+20	869	496
Jan 76	583	600½	579	600½	+20	860	503
Mar	590	607	588½	607	+20	620	511
SOYBEAN OIL							
May	29.00	29.90	28.80	29.90b	+1.00	45.88	20.60
July	27.80	28.63	27.65	28.63b	+1.00	45.12	22.45
Aug	26.95	27.55	26.75	27.55b	+1.00	44.30	21.90
Sept	26.00	26.72	25.85	26.72b	+1.00	43.70	21.15
Oct	24.90	25.50	24.80	25.50b	+1.00	32.75	20.32
Dec	23.80	24.60	23.75	24.60b	+1.00	30.90	19.60
Jan 76	23.25	24.10	23.25	24.10b	+1.00	28.50	19.25
Mar	23.00	23.60	22.90	23.60b	+1.00	23.60	19.20
SOYBEAN MEAL							
May	127.50	132.00	127.50	131.70 132.	+3.5to3.8	218.50	106.50
July	133.00	136.50	132.00	135.50	+2.70	212.50	112.00
Aug	135.00	138.50	134.50	138.50	+3.80	212.00	115.00
Sept	137.50	141.50	136.00	141.50	+5.00	211.00	118.00
Oct	140.00	143.50	138.50	143.00b	+5.00	170.00	121.50
Dec	142.50	146.00	140.00	144.00 143.	+3.5to2.5	166.00	124.00
Jan 76	142.50	148.00	141.50	145.50 145.	+4.2to3.7	169.00	124.00
Mar	145.00	148.00	144.00	147.00b	+1.50	151.00	133.50
ICED BROILERS							
May	40.05	40.62	40.00	40.60	+ .50	46.65	36.00
June	40.00	40.45	40.00	40.40 45	+ .40to.45	46.50	36.85
July	39.95	40.40	39.95	40.30	+ .45	46.50	37.00
Aug	39.75	39.90	39.70	39.90	+ .40	43.00	37.10
Sept	38.75	39.00	38.70	38.75	+ .35	42.50	35.75
Nov	37.00	37.50	37.00	37.50b	+ .50	39.25	35.65
PLYWOOD							
May	132.60	134.60	131.20	132.50 .30	+ .60to.40	134.60	100.00
July	135.50	137.50	134.00	135.20 135.	+ .70to.50	137.50	102.00
Sept	138.00	130.00	137.00	137.50	+ .50	140.00	104.50
Nov	139.40	141.50	138.50	139.00	+ .10	141.50	115.00
Jan 76	143.50	143.50	141.00	141.00	+ .20	143.50	126.00
CHICAGO – SILVER							
Apr	422.00	427.00	419.00	426.00	+5.20	649.00	349.70
May	424.50	429.00	423.00	428.50b	+3.50	456.50	416.00
June	428.00	433.50	425.50	432.40 432	+5.4to5.0	653.00	395.00
Aug	432.50	438.50	431.00	438.00	+4.80	563.50	402.00
Oct	439.00	445.00	438.00	444.00	+5.00	570.00	405.00
Dec	444.50	452.50	444.00	450.00	+5.70	574.00	410.00
Feb 76	452.00	456.00	451.00	456.00	+6.00	506.00	430.00
Apr	458.00	462.00	457.00	461.50	S6.30	512.00	437.50
June	467.00	467.00	467.00	467.00	S6.50	500.00	454.00
KANSAS CITY – WHEAT							
May	368	375	368	373 371½	+8to6½	539½	328
July	368	374	368	373-372	+8¼to7¼	509¾	331
Sept	374	378½	373	377	+8	489	336½
Dec	380	385	380	385	+7½	409	348
MINNEAPOLIS – WHEAT							
May	406	413	406	411	+6½	576	373
July	398	402	397	401a	+7	560	361
Sept	386	393	386	392a	+7	453	360
Dec	395	398	395	398b	+8	393	395
WINNIPEG – RAPESEED (VANCOUVER)							
June	696	706	696	706b	+20	974	524
Sept	681	691	681	691b	+20	930	520
Nov	665	668	665	668b	+20	684	510¼
RYE							
May	219½	227	219	227b	+10	363¾	191
July	218½	226¼	218¼	226¼b	+10	364	185¾
OATS							
May	168	169½	168	169½	+1½	213½	143½
July	154	158	154	158a	+4	197	140¼
						330	221

	Open	High	Low	Close	Change	Season's High	Season's Low
CATTLE (CHICAGO – MERCANTILE EXCHANGE)							
Apr	40.20	41.20	40.12	40.90 .95	+ .30to.35	50.70	33.75
[illegible]	[illegible]	41.87	40.30	41.87 .80	+ .92to.85	50.40	35.17
[illegible]	[illegible]	[illegible]	38.75	40.22 .17	+ .80to.75	50.60	34.85
[illegible]	[illegible]	[illegible]	37.90	39.30	+ .95	43.50	34.27
[illegible]	[illegible]	[illegible]	37.65	39.35	+1.25	42.00	34.35
[illegible]	[illegible]	[illegible]	37.65	39.20	+1.05	39.60	34.52
…0,419 contracts.							
[illegible]	[illegible]	40.45	39.40	39.40	.55	62.50	39.40
May	41.05	41.75	41.00	41.50-.45	+ .35to.30	60.95	40.15
[illegible]	42.00	42.95	42.00	42.70-.45	+ .55to.30	61.00	40.70
[illegible]	[illegible]	51.85	50.55	51.45 -	+ .55	55.00	49.50
…ted at: 427 contracts.							
…(IDAHO RUSSET)							
[illegible]	[illegible]	5.05	5.05	5.05	+ .05	10.10	4.91
…ntracts.							
…EN PORK BELLIES							
May	69.60	71.82	69.45	71.82b	+1.50	72.70	36.25
July	70.00	72.35	70.00	72.35b	+1.50	73.00	38.25
Aug	68.70	70.85	68.70	70.85b	+1.50	72.00	52.10
Feb76	65.00	66.50	65.00	66.50b	+1.50	72.80	55.25
Mar	66.25	66.35	66.25	66.35b	+1.50	66.35	58.70
May	66.50	67.50	66.50	67.50b	no comp	67.50	66.50
Sales estimated at: 5,443 contracts.							
HOGS							
Apr	41.40	42.45	41.35	42.40 .35	+ .68to.63	48.50	26.30
June	44.30	45.90	44.30	45.85-.90	+1.28to1.33	49.90	35.30
July	45.30	46.80	45.25	46.75-.80	+1.03to1.08	51.10	36.72
Aug	44.60	46.00	44.50	45.95-46.	+1.05to1.10	49.40	39.00
Oct	43.80	45.10	43.70	45.00-.10	+ .95to1.05	47.80	38.70
Dec	43.85	45.50	43.85	45.40-.50	+1.28to1.38	48.00	38.75
Feb76	43.20	44.60	43.20	44.40-.60	+1.00to1.20	44.60	38.30
Apr	41.95	43.35	41.80	43.25b	+1.40	43.35	38.00
Sales estimated at: 4,832 contracts.							
LUMBER							
May	136.00	138.00	134.80	134.80-135.	1.0to.80	145.80	107.10
July	151.00	153.80	148.50	148.50-.50	2.3to2.6	152.00	111.00
Sept	157.10	159.00	155.40	155.50	2.00	159.00	127.50
Nov	155.50	158.10	153.10	153.20-.20	3.2to3.3	158.10	140.00
Sales estimated at: 1,678 contracts.							
NEW YORK – SILVER							
Apr	424.50	427.50	424.50	427.40	+4.40	468.50	417.50
May	426.50	421.50	425.00	420.00	+4.50	657.00	342.90
July	431.00	435.90	429.00	435.90	+4.90	659.40	400.00
Sept	436.00	442.00	425.00	441.60	+5.00	650.10	407.10
Dec	446.00	451.50	444.00	450.20	+5.10	568.00	417.00
Jan76	446.50	452.80	446.50	452.80	+5.20	572.00	419.00
Mar	452.50	458.40	452.50	458.40	+5.20	576.00	433.00
May	453.00	463.90	458.00	463.90	+5.20	529.00	440.00
July	464.00	470.00	464.00	469.30	+5.20	500.00	459.40
Sales estimated at: 4,623 contracts.							
COPPER							
Apr	61.40	61.40	61.40	61.40	+ .70	61.40	52.50
May	61.40	62.00	61.40	61.90	+ .70	126.20	52.50
July	62.30	63.00	62.30	62.90	+ .70	103.50	53.70
Sept	63.30	64.00	63.30	64.00	+ .80	96.00	55.00
Dec	65.10	65.80	65.10	65.60	+ .70	74.20	56.50
Jan76	65.70	66.30	65.70	66.10	+ .70	67.00	57.50
Mar	66.60	67.20	66.60	67.00	+ .70	68.00	58.50
Sales estimated at: 639 contracts.							
SUGAR (WORLD CONTRACT)							
May	24.05	25.30	23.60	24.95-25.3	unch to+.40	63.44	7.80
July	23.35	24.60	22.60	24.00-.60	+ .10to.70	61.05	10.20
Sept	22.05	23.50	21.70	22.9-23.5	+ .05to.65	56.05	10.40
Oct	21.80	22.60	21.80	22.30-.60	+ .20to.50	53.55	11.95
Mar76	19.80	20.50	19.40	20.20-.50	.10to+.20	45.45	19.40
May	19.40	20.00	18.95	19.90-20.	+ .10to.20	28.65	18.95
July	18.90	18.90	18.40	19.45n	+ .10	25.10	18.40
Sales: 4,532 contracts. Spot: 24.00n.							
COFFEE							
July	52.25	52.64	52.20	52.60	+ .10to.14	66.55	50.70
Sept	53.80	54.25	53.40	54.10-.25	+ .40to.55	63.55	51.30
Nov	53.90	54.30	53.90	54.60a	+ .60	63.50	53.10
Dec	54.15	54.60	53.90	54.60	+ .44	64.05	52.75
Mar76	54.50	55.25	54.50	55.25	+ .25	55.35	51.60
Sales: 168 contracts							
COCOA							
May	62.25	62.35	61.25	61.55	–1.19	77.70	43.80
July	59.15	59.15	58.35	58.60	–1.15	73.50	46.40
Sept	57.75	57.80	57.25	57.65	– .90	70.00	48.70
Dec	56.70	56.75	56.30	56.55	– .80	66.45	52.00
Mar76	55.90	55.90	55.41	55.65	– .75	64.20	51.00
Sales: 1,395 contracts.							
WOOL FUTURES							
May	116.0	116.0	116.0	114.0b	......	215.0	99.0
July	121.0	121.0	121.0	119.0b	......	198.0	102.0
Dec	126.0	126.0	126.0	123.0b	+2.0	139.5	104.0
Spot: 105.0n.							
ORANGE JUIC[illegible]NCENTRATED)							
						60.85	47.50

Jan. 27 . . . . 3.13
Jan. 28 . . . . 3.17½
Jan. 29 . . . . 3.21½
Jan. 30 . . . . 3.17½

Step One: With the 8½-inch sides of your graph paper as top and bottom, write the name and month of your commodity in the upper right corner of the paper. Draw two lines at right angles about an inch for the side and bottom as shown below. These are the *price line* and the *date line*.

Figure 12

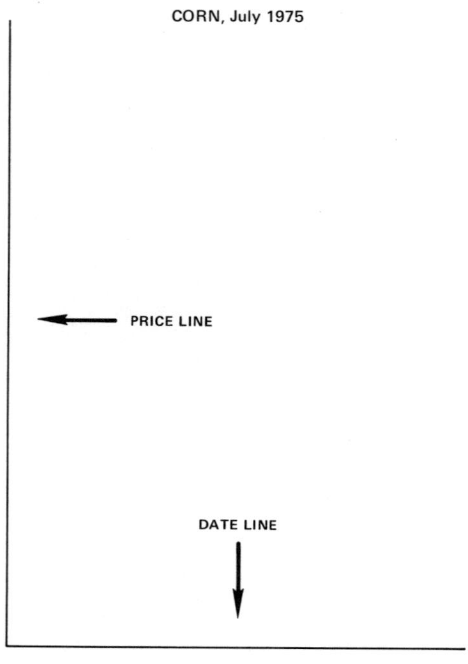

Step Two: Take the lowest price of your ten day price range and place it on a line about one inch above the Date Line and to the left of the price line (If the price has a fraction, leave it off). Then, place a price on every line in increments of one cent* to fill out the Price Line above and below the lowest price you have just entered. If the highest price in your range goes beyond the top of your graph, add another sheet by taping the edges together on the reverse side, matching the lines on the front side, and continue the Price line. The lowest price in my July corn sample is $3.05-3/4.

*One verticle square per one cent is used for grains (wheat, corn, oats, soybeans) because their minimum fluctuation is ¼ of a cent. Other commodities have varying minimum fluctuations. You would use more squares per one cent if the fluctuations are very small, or each square might equal 10*c* or more. A good rule is to use about 10 squares per daily limit move.

Figure 13

CORN, July 1975

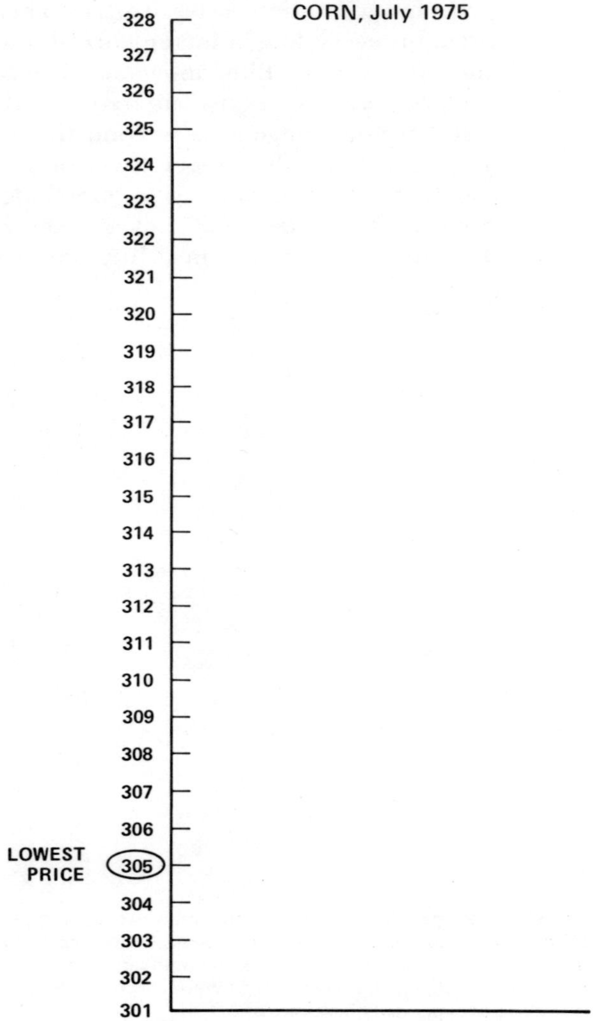

Step Three: Along the Date Line write in the dates of the ten previous trading days you have listed. Each square should equal two trading days, so write the first date on the first line and the next date in the space between the first and second line, etc.

Figure 14

CORN, July 1975

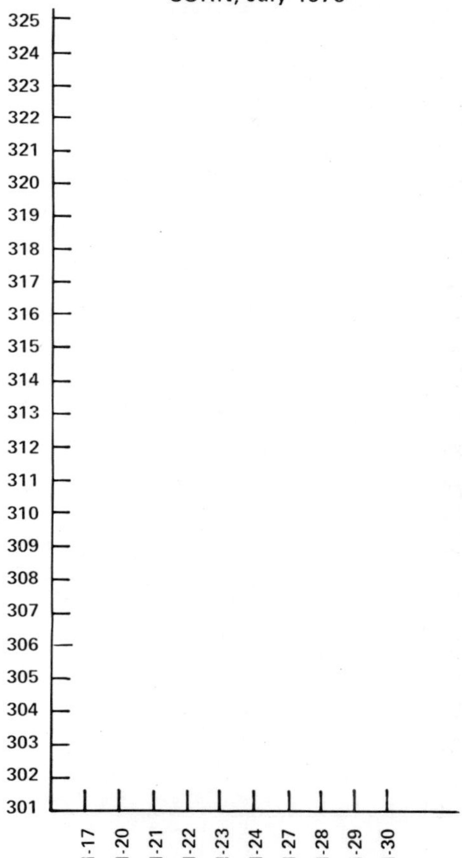

Step Four: Plot the ten days' closing prices on the chart by placing a small dot at the intersection of the date and the price. I have plotted the July corn prices below.

Figure 15

CORN, July 1975

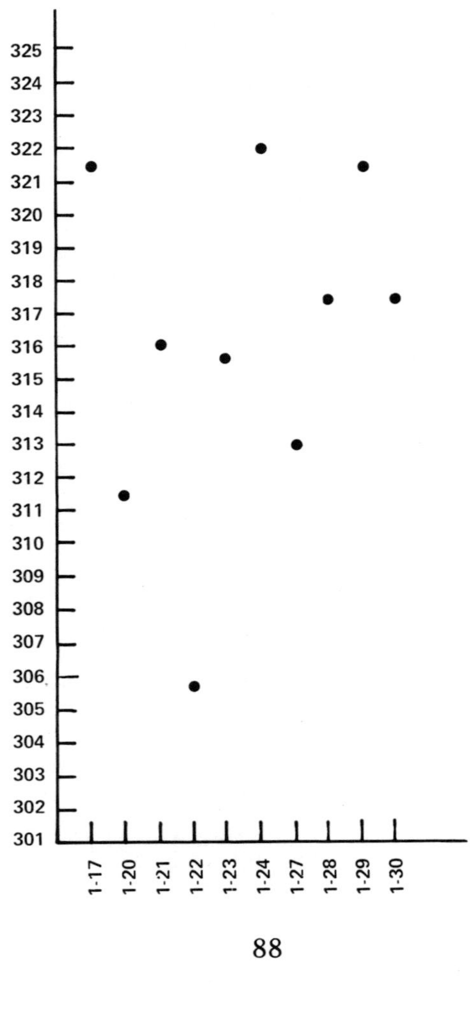

Step Five: Connect the dots with a ruler as illustrated below.

Figure 16

CORN, July 1975

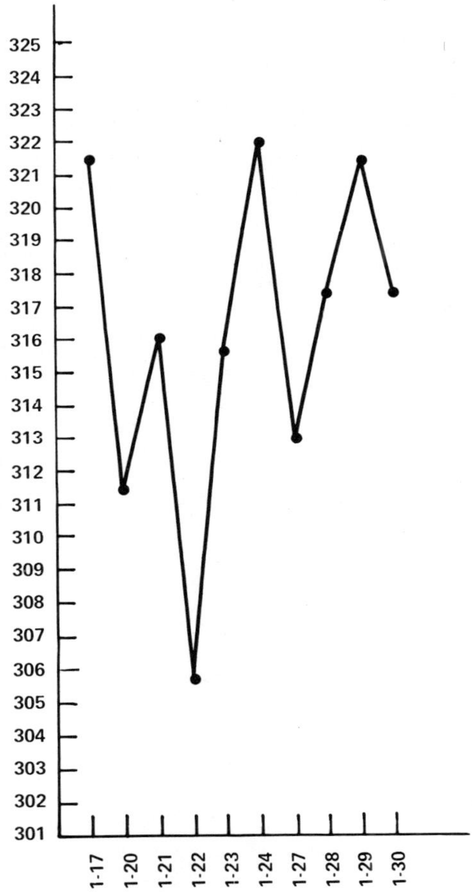

When these five steps are completed, you are ready to plot "today's" closing price and each subsequent closing price for as long as you trade in that commodity.

When required, additional sheets of graph paper can be added to any side of the original chart by matching the lines and taping on the reverse side.

If you keep charts on other commodities besides the one you are currently interested in, you will be ready to switch to another commodity without rushing to make up a new chart. If you clip the Futures Prices from the paper, you will have a record of past prices when you wish to make additional charts.

The patterns formed by the connected dots in Step Five, reveal Congestion Phases which are explained in Chapter One of this book.

GLOSSARY

GLOSSARY OF COMMODITY TRADING TERMS

BEAR – A market "pessimist" who thinks prices will decline. Can refer to news as being "bearish," or a "bear" trend.

BEAR MARKET – A market in which prices are declining.

BREAK – A sharp decline in price.

BROKER – An agent entrusted to executive orders.

BULL – One who is optimistic about the market and thinks prices will go up. Can refer to a commodity or some news as "bullish."

BULL MARKET – A market in which prices are rising.

CASH COMMODITY– A commodity available for immediate sale and delivery.

CLEARING-HOUSE – An association of exchange member firms through which financial settlements between traders are made.

CLOSE – The minutes at the end of each trading session during which all trades are officially declared executed "on the close."

COMMISSION – The fee charged by a broker for the execution of customer orders.

COMMISSION HOUSE– A firm which buys and sells commodity contracts for customers. Also called a brokerage firm or house.

CONGESTION – A period of relative stability in market prices, defined by temporary price range.

CONTRACT – The unit of trading for commodity transactions, specifying the quantity to be bought or sold.

DELIVERY MONTH– The month during which a contract expires, and delivery is made.

FARM PRICES – Prices actually received by farmers for their products as reported by the Department of Agriculture.

FLOOR BROKER – A person who executes buy and sell orders for others in exchange for a fee.

FLOOR TRADER – An exchange members who trades for himself personally on the exchange floor.

FUNDAMENTAL ANALYSIS– A major trading method of evaluating evaluating such factors as crop and weather reports, supply and demand variables, politics, etc., in order to predict price fluctuations.

FUTURES CONTRACT– An agreement to buy or sell a com-commodity at a future date under specific, standardized terms.

HEDGING – A technique used by industry to protect itself from future price decline or rise by either purchasing futures contracts against anticipated requirements or selling the equivalent in futures contracts of physical commodity as protection against a price decline.

JOB LOT – A unit of trading usually 1,000 or 2,000 bushels.

LIMIT – The maximum price advance or decline from the previous day's closing price permitted in one day of trading.

LIMITED ORDER – One in which the customer sets a limit on the price he will trade at.

LONG – One who has bought a contract or a position in the market of having bought.

MAINTENANCE MARGIN– The amount of money required to ed to sustain a position without a margin call, once it has been entered into. This amount is usually less than the initial margin requirement.

MARGIN – The money deposited as a "show of good faith" by a trader to ensure fulfillment of a contract. It is a performance bond, rather than a down payment, as in a stock transaction.

MARGIN CALL – An order by which a brokerage firm may request additional funds from a trader to restore the maintenance margin when losses have depleted the margin already deposited.

MARKET ORDER – An order that is to be filled as soon as possible at whatever the price is at that time.

MECHANICAL METHOD— A trading method in which rigid, step-by-step trading rules are followed.

LONG TERM — When futures contracts are held for six months or longer in order to qualify for a substantial tax break on profits.

OPENING or OPEN — The official start of the trading day.

OPENING RANGE — In open auction with many buyers and sellers, contracts are traded at several prices at the opening of the market.

OPEN INTEREST — The total of unfilled contracts on one side of the market.

PAPER PROFIT — Profit which would be realized if contracts were liquidated at a specific time and price.

PIT — Designated locations on the trading floor of an exchange where futures trading takes place. Pits are designated for specific commodities.

POSITION — Whether a trader is long or short is his position. If he is not long or short he has no position in the market.

P & S STATEMENT – The Purchase and Sale Statement sent by the broker to customers when a position has changed or a trade completed.

RALLY – A price movement upward caused by buying in the market.

RANDOM WALK – A theory of price fluctuation based on the law of probability.

REACTION – A downward movement in prices following an advance, or rally.

RISK AVERSION – A theory of emotional bias in traders.

RECOVERY – Advance of prices after a decline.

ROUND LOT – A 5,000 bushel contract.

SCALPER, SCALPING– A speculator, operating on the trading trading floor who privides market liquidity by rapidly buying and selling for small profits.

SETTLEMENT PRICE– The price at the end of the trading session at which the Clearing House clears all trades of the day.

SHORT – When a trader initiates a position

by selling a contract, i.e., the selling side of an open contract.

SPECULATOR— A trader who attempts to anticipate price changes and make profits through market activities.

SPOT COMMODITY— See Cash Commodity.

SPLIT-CLOSE— When there are two closing prices that vary slightly. The settlement price will be the average between the two.

SPREAD— Also called a "Straddle," it is the purchase of one future contract against the sale of another of the same commodity, or of different commodities. The difference between the two prices is the profit.

STOP ORDER— An order to buy or sell when the price reaches a specific point. When the stop price is reached the stop order then becomes a market order.

STRAIGHT-AWAY— A strong movement in one direction after a price has stabilized for a short time in a period of congestion.

TRADING LIMIT–	See "Limit."
TREND–	The direction prices are going.
VOLUME OF TRADING–	The amount of sales and purchases of a commodity during a specific period of time. The sales and purchases are equivalent.